THE TRANSFOI
OF THE IRISH
1550–1700

RAYMOND GILLESPIE

Printed by
DUNDALGAN PRESS (W. Tempest) LTD.
1991

ISSN No. 0790–2913
ISBN No. 0 947897 04 6

INTRODUCTION

'The economic and social history of Ireland before 1660', L.M. CULLEN (1976) has written 'is obscure'. While the later part of the seventeenth century is not in complete darkness, it too is veiled by a heavy mist. One reason for this is the unpromising nature of the historical sources. Yet English historians have shown that 'in the last resort, perhaps the darkness of the sixteenth and seventeenth centuries depends on the angle from which they are approached and upon the questions that are asked about them'.[1] Many aspects of early modern Ireland, notably its constitutional status, its political development and its religious structures, have been subjected to new questions and different approaches in recent years, but economic life remains largely untouched. The most eloquent testimony to this neglect is that the last general book on the subject, that by George O'BRIEN, was published in 1919. Given the political environment in which that survey was written it is not surprising that O'Brien's analysis assumed a strong malevolent intent in English economic policy towards early modern Ireland.

The neglect of socio-economic history has given rise to a distorted view of the social revolution which occurred in Ireland between 1550 and 1700. Ireland before that period, as described by D.B. QUINN and K.W. NICHOLLS, was a society fragmented in economic, political and social terms. It was composed of a large number of power blocks, the influence of which fluctuated widely according to the capacity of individual lords to command support. The region of English influence, the 'pale' in the east, was made up at that stage of two geographically distinct parts. The northern pale extended from Dublin to Dundalk and west to the borders of the modern counties of Laois and Offaly, and was separated from the southern pale, based on Waterford and Wexford, by the lordship of the O'Byrnes and the Wicklow mountains. This region of English influence can be broken down in other ways, such as an inner pale around Dublin dominated by many small land-owners, and an outer pale dominated by the much larger lordships of the earls of Kildare and Ormond. A manorial type of economy and an inheritance system based on primogeniture was the norm throughout this region. The trade of the pale was dominated by large towns of which the most important were Dublin (described recently by Colm LENNON) and Drogheda. Little evidence survives for the distribution of wealth within the pale region but the sixteenth-century ecclesiastical valuations of benefices calculated by Steven ELLIS point to a concentration of wealth around the Dublin and Meath areas, followed closely by Louth. Of the south eastern dioceses Ferns was the wealthiest, although the average benefice there was worth only half of its Dublin equivalent, with the values of benefices falling in the dioceses of Cashel and Leighlin as the native Irish regions were approached.

Outside the pale, in the area of Gaelic influence, were many small, more or less independent lordships which in the early Tudor period were in a continual state of fragmentation and reconstruction. Here political and economic power fluctuated in accordance with military might. Land was held by freeholders under a lord, rather than in great estates as in the pale. The consequences of this contrast will be examined later. The Gaelic areas were characterised by a general lack of towns; the few ports of any size, Cork and Galway for example, were dominated by the Anglo-Irish. By contrast with the east of the country, coinage was in much less general use in these areas. However coin was used and in one case, that of the O'Reillys, an Irish lord struck his own coin. The evidence of coin hoards from the west suggests that the link between the metalic value of the coin and its value for trade was not as well developed in Gaelic Ireland as in the pale. Base coin, for instance, seems to have circulated longer and seventeenth-century hoards often contain sixteenth-century base coin.

While it is fairly easy to draw a picture of these two regions it is much more difficult to identify the border between them. Areas such as the modern counties of Longford and Cavan, which in ethnic terms should belong to the Gaelic region had close economic and social links with the pale through trade and elite marriage alliances and these contacts were of profound importance in their later development. The border areas were, however, a relatively small part of the story and broadly speaking two contrasting regions and two sharply divided types of society co-existed in early sixteenth-century Ireland.

Trends in the sixteenth-century economy

Detailed evidence on sixteenth-century economic activity, whether archaeological, manorial, municipal financial or fiscal, is expectionally thin compared with other European countries, or compared with Ireland in the following century. Such evidence as does exist has not been fully sifted by historians. Sixteenth-century customs data, for example, are fragmentary and rendered almost useless by the exemptions given by the government to the port towns and to individuals, as Victor TREADWELL (1977) has shown. Trade data gathered from the English port books by LONGFIELD is also of limited value; the portion of the sixteenth-century economy involved in foreign trade was relatively small because of the uncommercialised nature of that economy. The main port towns were located in the commercialised coastal areas of the east and south of the country rather than in Gaelic Ireland where trading was conducted through local harbours. Robert Coggan's report on Irish trade in 1611 is probably equally applicable to the late sixteenth century.[2] At that time Dublin, trading largely with England, was by far the largest town with trade worth £80,000 a year. Next was Waterford with a trade of £30,000 a year made up of exports of corn, frieze, tallow, hides and pipe-staves, trading mainly with Spain and on the return journey bringing wine, iron and salt to Bristol before purchasing goods there for Ireland. The value of the trade of both Galway and Cork, mainly with Spain, was estimated at about £20,000 a year, as was that of Drogheda. The trade of Limerick and Wexford was valued at £10,000 and £4,000 a year respectively.

Political factors which restricted Irish trade during the sixteenth century, particularly in the 1560s and 1570s, also make trade records an unreliable guide. Grain, for example, rarely features in the port books before 1603, but this reflects the penal customs duties levied by the crown rather than a low level of Irish grain production. Similarly cattle and beef feature only occasionally in the port books, yet according to one account of 1569 Spanish fishermen at Cork purchased 2,000 cattle along with hides and tallow.

Much of the evidence from Gaelic Ireland is drawn from the duties paid to overlords from their followers. These sources reveal an economy dominated largely by livestock but with much more grain being produced than historians have hitherto suspected. The goods left behind by the earl of Tyrone when he left Ireland in 1607 included 300 sheep, 240 barrels of butter, 200 barrels of oats, 120 barrels of oatmeal and 72 pigs. Those of his followers who accompanied him left 172 cattle, 82 sheep, 57 horses and 120 pigs. There were also about 6,000 cattle on the lands of Tyrone's followers. However these represented only moveable goods. Frequent references to the burning of grain in the later years of the Nine Years War suggest that large quantities of grain must have been grown in Ulster. Some quantification of the relative importance of the various sectors of the agricultural economy is possible in the case of the O'Duinn territory in the northern part of county Laois. Using contemporary valuations the renders to the lord comprised 52 per cent cattle or beef, 24 per cent butter, and 19 per cent in grain or bread. Again losses reported by the earl of Ormond in 1567 included 9,875 cattle, 4,458 pigs, 9,841 sheep and 2,827 plough horses suggesting a considerable area under the plough. In the midlands during the late sixteenth century the exaction of agricultural labour services suggests that at least some of this grain was grown as part of demesne agriculture. However it is clear that at least the midlands were not self-sufficient in grain production, for in years of harvest crisis, such as 1556, 1557 and 1560, palesmen were prohibited by proclamation from selling grain to the native Irish in adjacent territories.

It is difficult to describe the regional variations in sixteenth-century agriculture. It seems that in Munster sheep were more important than cattle. Certainly during the Desmond rebellion seizures of sheep were considerably greater than those of cattle and it was from Munster that most of the wool and woollen cloth shipped to England originated. Bristol, for example, imported some 26,556 yards in 1559/60. The range of the Munster economy is probably reflected in the imports to the ports of southern England studied by LONGFIELD: hides (some tanned and others salted), wool, frieze (a low grade woollen cloth), tallow, fish and timber. Timber was a growing trade in the sixteenth century, first appearing in the English port books in the 1550s and expanding dramatically in the late sixteenth century. To this must also be added considerable grain production which was not reflected in the recorded trade. Fish were important along the west coast and salmon was traded regularly for wine by the Ulster lords, One growing element in the economy of the northern part of Ireland in the late sixteenth century was linen yarn. The exports of Irish linen yarn to Liverpool, one of the main ports receiving the northern Irish trade, grew from 356 packs in 1565/6 to 1,555 packs in 1593/4. Wool exports also grew in the same period from 630 stone to 1,506 stone, but it was linen yarn which was the more important export to Liverpool being valued in 1592/4 at £7,552. 10s. against wool exports of £424.13s. A similar, though less dramatic rise, has been shown for Chester by Donald WOODWARD (1970a). Much of this wool and linen was woven into cloth around Manchester where, according to one account, some 4,000 people were employed working Irish yarn in the mid-sixteenth century. Production of linen yarn on this scale would be consistent with an economy which depended mainly on livestock and which required little regular labour, hence the available labour force had the time, if not always the incentive, to produce other goods such as linen yarn.

One feature common to all the economic regions of sixteenth-century Ireland was a lack of either regional specialisation or diversification. One of the peculiarities of the sixteenth-century economy was that while increasing amounts of yarn and wool were being exported, cloth imports grew to supplement local production. Robert Coggan commented in 1611, for example, that linen yarn and wool were among the main exports of Dublin and that linen and woollen cloth were among its principal imports. The Irish economy did not have the native skills to process its raw materials. Similarly, one of the most profitable areas of the Irish economy in the sixteenth century, fishing, was almost entirely in the hands of foreigners. The same was true of mining as O'SULLIVAN's study of sixteenth-century mining in Ireland has shown.

Part of the explanation for this was a skill scarcity in sixteenth-century Ireland. Edmund Tremayne, for example, commented in

1571 that Ireland was very short of 'artificers' except around Waterford. Certainly the pardons issued to the followers of O'Connor Sligo after the Nine Years War reveal that of 990 persons only 26 described themselves as craftsmen. The two largest groups were agricultural workers, 335 persons, and soldiers of various types, 311 persons. This reflects the low population and the easy availability of land which reduced the need to diversify skills beyond what was required to maintain agricultural production. The fact that the society was little commercialised meant that specialised production of craft items for a wider market was very limited. Also, as many seventeenth-century commentators noted, the role of the craftsman was a lowly one. Weavers, for example, were regarded as of very low status indeed. Gaelic Ireland was a society articulated by warfare and those who did not take part in such warfare were marginalised. Moreover social norms were not geared to the capital investment required to develop fishing or mining. The income of the great Gaelic lords was not usually received in money rents but mainly in the form of entertainment or food. Society was thus organised around consumption rather than capital investment.

Attempts were made, especially in the pale and the port towns, to improve this situation. In 1555, for instance, Dublin corporation decreed that merchants should not import anything that could be made locally. Attempts were also made as part of plantation schemes to introduce new trades and crops. The cultivation of woad and madder as a source of dyes for the cloth trade, for example, was advocated as part of the Munster plantation to provide employment. Perhaps the most sustained attempt to diversify the economy came in Lord Deputy Sidney's viceroyalty. Sidney himself was keen to effect local economic change and was instrumental in settling a group of Flemish tanners at Swords, near Dublin, in the 1570s. On a broader level at the parliament of 1569-71, described by TREADWELL (1966-7), a strategy to encourage manufactures in Ireland was adopted so that processed goods rather than raw materials would be exported. Customs duties were to be increased and idle men, thought to be the root of disturbances, would be given profitable work. The legislation of the parliament included attempts to improve the quality of Irish tanning by licensing tanners and prohibiting the export of linen yarn in the hope that it would be worked up into cloth at home. In the short term this may have had some success but the problems of skill and capital shortages meant that it had little long-term effect. Furthermore, the impact of such legislation on Gaelic Ireland was negligible since the native Irish population were little influenced by offical English attitudes in their trade with France or Spain.

The lack of diversification or regional specialisation does not seem to have retarded the sixteenth-century Irish economy unduly. The evidence is scant but the few indications which exist all point to economic improvement in the late sixteenth century. Tax receipts excluding arrears, for example, rose by almost a fifth between the early 1580s and the outbreak of the Nine Years War (although this may reflect administrative efficiency as much as an improving economic performance). Other indicators also suggest a strong economy. The evidence of the coin hoards, for instance, suggests a large influx of English coin with a high silver content in the 1570s and 1580s. The Irish pound's exchange rate with sterling remained relatively stable between 1561 and 1600 despite the evidence from the English port books that Irish imports grew in volume and range over the period. At Chester in the early 1580s, for instance, recorded exports to Ireland were more than three times the value of recorded imports from Ireland using official valuations. Such a growth in imports also indicates greater prosperity at home. At least some of this favourable picture can be ascribed to the remarkable price stability, demonstrated by CULLEN, SMOUT and GIBSON, which seems to have prevailed in late sixteenth-century Ireland. While evidence for price movements is scant, the corporation book of the Irishtown of Kilkenny, for example, shows little movement during the late sixteenth century in local Irish prices. Many contemporaries commented favourably on the low level of Irish prices. By contrast England in the second half of the sixteenth century saw unprecedented inflation generated in part by population growth which placed a strain on resources, and by the inflow of precious metals which, when turned into coin, increased the money supply. Neither of these elements were features of the late sixteenth-century Irish economy. Population in Ireland remained low in relation to land

and Ireland, not having a mint, could not directly increase its money supply. The result was a low inflationary economy beside a high inflationary one which gave Ireland a considerable competitive advantage over one of its main trading partners. However such an analysis must remain speculative given the scarcity of evidence with which to work.

The competitive advantage of low inflation may have been significant in the commercialised areas of the pale but the argument may have less validity in Gaelic Ireland. There economic life was carried on in a much less commercial way and was outside the sphere of offically recorded commercial activity. It may be that the apparent prosperity represents rather a transfer of wealth within Gaelic Ireland. As great native lords used techniques such as surrender and regrant to reduce the status of their freeholders to tenants they were able to increase the duties received from them. In this way wealth, and hence purchasing power, passed from freeholder to lord who then purchased luxury items, such as wine, abroad.

The history of the following century and a half is centered on a social revolution which replaced the variety of social, economic and political systems of sixteenth-century Ireland with a single one modelled on early modern England. As one contemporary put it, the native Irish were to 'grow into a body commoned and into a commonwealth whereas before they wholly consisted of poor proud gentry'[3]—a reference to the fragmented Irish lordships which had little contact with a market economy. One of the ways in which this commonwealth would grow, according to contemporary social theorists, was through economic development. Making the native Irish wealthy would give them a stake in the country and they would then be reluctant to compromise their new found wealth by rebellion. It would also introduce them to the language of commerce, English, and so remove the cultural barrier of the Irish language which prevented their full assimilation with the settler community in Ireland.

The mechanism by which this was to be achieved was the introduction in part or en bloc of many of the elements of English commercial organisation and landholding. Thus the framework of a contract between landlord and tenant would provide a check on the power formerly exerised by the great native Irish lords who, the English believed, had oppressed their followers and agricultural dependants who had never had fixity of tenure on the lands they worked. The introduction of new settlers, mainly English and Scots, through plantation and more informal colonisation, would bring English styles of agriculture, especially labour-intensive tillage, and this, it was argued, would provide employment for the 'idle' Irish who had previously spent their time plotting rebellion.

Early modern governments could plan such extensive schemes for social change with ease, but it proved far more difficult to execute them. There was no abundant supply of settlers with sufficient capital and enthusiasm to people the projected plantations. In particular, government ambition to extend tillage proved impractical given Ireland's climate and soil which was best suited to livestock production. Thus the economic survival of a plantation settlement could only be assured by reversing one rationale for its existence.

The main agent of economic change turned out to be not the state but the land-owning class. Yet the actions of landlords were themselves determined by a variety of influences: the demands of government, local environmental conditions, the demands of their tenants, the need for profit and the fluctuating commercial opportunities presented by an expanding economy. This essay is an attempt to examine how the different forces for change operated and interacted in the late sixteenth and seventeenth centuries. First, we will examine the long-term changes within the Irish economy: the rapid growth in population, the redistribution of resources and the commercialisation of the economy and its partial integration into a widening world of maritime trade. Secondly, we will look at the short term changes in the economy in order to discover the timing of change and the role of such factors as price movements and individual landlord initiatives. Finally, we will consider the limits which were set on economic change both as a result of non-economic factors, such as legislation and the physical environment, and institutional factors such as the financial system.

THE DYNAMICS OF CHANGE

Among the three long-term forces shaping economic change in early modern Ireland—the growth of population, the internal redistribution of resources and a dramatic commercialisation of the economy—the growth in population was probably the most significant. Population growth meant a growth in the supply of labour and hence increased output. There were of course other ways of increasing output such as the introduction of new agricultural techniques, but frequently these were to prove expensive to introduce and poorly adapted to local conditions. In many cases indigenous Irish agricultural techniques, such as attaching the plough to the horse's tail, were adopted by the British settlers. Where land-use change occurred, it was generally increased labour which prompted such change. An increased labour supply meant that more land could be utilised and land already being exploited could be used more intensively thus achieving an increase in productivity. A rise in agricultural output ahead of rapid population growth was possible because of the very low levels of sixteenth-century Irish population. The marginal return on labour remained high as population growth accelerated in the seventeenth century. Even late in that century when much of the dramatic change in the economy was over, Sir Robert Southwell saw output increasing in line with population growth, contending 'that in twelve years Ireland would be double in value because of double hands'.[4]

I

It is not possible to quantify with any accuracy the population totals in early modern Ireland because the first figures of any value only become available in the 1670s. L.M. CULLEN (1974-5) has proposed a series of plausible estimates of Irish population between 1500 and 1700.

TABLE I

Irish Population Estimates, 1500-1712

Year	Inhabitants (millions)	Growth Rate (per cent per annum)
1500	1.0	-
1600	1.4	0.3
1641	2.1	1.0
1672	1.7	0.6
1687	2.2	1.7
1712	2.8	0.9

Source: CULLEN (1974-5)

Cullen's earlier figures may require some downward adjustments (for example the estimate for 1500 should probably be lowered to between 0.5 million and 0.75 million), but nevertheless these estimates reflect the broad trend of population change. The sixteenth-century growth rate is within the 'normal' European pre-industrial pattern with immigration having only a slight effect. Indeed the plantation of Munster, according to Michael MacCarthy Morrogh's (1986) estimates, added only about 3,000 people to the region by 1592. This in-migration may well have been balanced by Irish emigration, especially to England and Wales; this would be a normal movement from a relatively poor area to a more wealthy one. George Owen's description of Pembrokeshire in 1603 noted that 'as for the Irishmen they are so powdered among the inhabitants of Roose and Castlemartin that in every village you shall find the third, fourth and fifth household-er an Irishman... they are so increased that there are some whole parishes inhabited by the Irish'.[5] These settlers, noted Owen, came mainly from south-west Ireland. This example was not unusual. The English vagrancy act of 1572 mentioned the Irish as a particu-lar problem, and arrests for vagrancy within England in the late sixteenth century included significant numbers of Irish. In London three per cent of arrests in 1574-9 were Irish, increasing to eight per cent in 1604-10, and the proportion was even greater on the west coast of England. Irish names also occur as apprentices in sixteenth-century London, demonstrating the existence of a more settled Irish community there.

The sixteenth-century population of Ireland was not evenly spread across the country. There were areas of dense settlement, notably in parts of the pale where there was considerable competition for land rather than, as elsewhere, for men to work it. Indeed the pressure on land was so great that it was said that the pale lords could treat tenants almost as they wished 'suffering no tenant to have assurance underneath him but until another will give him more'.[6] The Ormond lordship in County Tipperary also seems to have been well settled, and according to a 1586 survey for the Munster plantation 80 to 90 per cent of county Limerick was populated. The southern parts of Munster seem to have had a much lower population density in the late sixteenth century if not earlier. Depopulation following the Desmond rebellion was at least partly responsible. To the north of Limerick, parts of Connacht also seem to have been fairly well populated to judge by the returns of composition rents, although late sixteenth-century English administrators considered the province to be underpopulated. It is clear that Ulster had by far the lowest population density in the late sixteenth century and there was a movement of tenants out of the pale to settle waste areas in south Ulster.

Irish population as a whole probably fell slightly in the 1590s as a result of both the Nine Years War and of migration from Munster to continental Europe and southern Britain. Recovery in the early seventeenth century was rapid, mainly due to the successful resettlement of Munster after the war. The opening up of Ulster and other Gaelic areas to immigration from England and Scotland by means of both official plantation schemes and more informal initiatives laid the basis for subsequent population growth. By the 1630s, when the Ulster population was at its pre-rebellion peak, there were about 15,000 settlers in that province alone. In Munster the settler population rose from about 5,000 in 1611 to almost 22,000 in 1641. Both here and in Ulster this growth began to taper off after the mid-1620s.

The motives which drew British settlers to Ireland have been analysed by GILLESPIE (1985) and MACCARTHY MORROGH (1986). Migrants were drawn from a wide cross section of English, Scottish and Welsh society. At the upper levels they included members of families who were rising and those who were declining on the social scale, the latter hoping to retrieve their fortunes and status by migration. At a lower social level cheap Irish land provided an attraction at a period when farm rents were rising rapidly in Scotland and in England. However, the magnetic pull of Ireland was soon reduced once the effects of the first generation of rapid population growth had worked its way through the system and opportunities were reduced. But the frontier of cheap land and economic opportunity shifted: many Ulster settlers migrated south and west as far as Longford and Sligo. In Munster, areas to the north of the formal plantation zone were settled by British families. However an apparently faster rate of population growth in Munster than in Ulster suggests that even with internal settler migrations there was a perceived shortage of local opportunity. As early as the 1620s there is evidence of emigration from Munster to America by recently arrived settlers and by native Irish. In particular, the expanding economy of the Caribbean provided an outlet for surplus Munster population. By the 1640s there was a substantial Irish community in St Christopher in Montserrat and by 1666 20 per cent of the population of Barbados was Irish in origin. The province of Munster also provided a fruitful recruiting ground for the Spanish armies, especially in the 1630s when continental warfare resumed. In addition there was a steady stream of Irish Catholics from all parts of the island travelling to continental colleges seeking the education denied to them at home; some did not return. It is difficult to measure the scale of this movement. In 1614 there were some 300 Irish students in France and Flanders and about 3,000 Irish soldiers in the Spanish army, while Arthur Chichester claimed in 1610 that he had sent 6,000 Ulster swordsmen to Sweden.

Despite this out-migration, early seventeenth-century demographic growth was very considerable. Much of it was lost in the 1640s and 1650s as a result of the catastrophic mixture of civil war and the plague which ravaged most of the country in 1649-53. According to Sir William Petty, 1,300 people in Dublin (perhaps three per cent of the city's population) were dying every week at the height of the outbreak. Plague affected urban areas worst so such a toll was not typical of the country as a whole but for affected communities the impact was shattering. The cumulative effect of almost ten years of war and plague, followed by 'famine fever' left about half the houses in Dublin deserted in the early 1650s. In Ulster a comparison of the surnames on the 1630 muster roll with the hearth-money rolls of the 1660s indicates that less that 50 per cent, and in some neighbourhoods less than 20 per cent, of 1630 surnames survived to the 1660s, indicating a huge turnover in population. In the early 1650s there was once again a considerable migration of Irish soldiers to serve in continental armies (about 30,000 according to some estimates). In addition there was the transportation of some Catholic Irish to the West Indies during that decade. From the mid-1650s immigration, to Ulster from northern England and Scotland began again, but the decade and a half of turmoil and crisis had been so severe across the country that it was probably not until the 1680s that Irish population regained the pre-1641 peak.

The immigration of the early seventeenth century had considerably changed the regional distribution of population within the island. William SMYTH has studied the 1660 pattern of settlement in detail. Ulster, the least densely settled of the four provinces at the end of the sixteenth century, was by then well settled. The east and north of the province, the areas closest to the supply of immigrants, were the most densely settled zones. North Leinster retained its very high population density, matched only by areas to the west of Cork city. Connacht, which seems to have had a reasonably dense population by Irish standards in the late sixteenth century, was falling behind in relative terms by 1660, in part because it was farthest away from the centres of primary immigration.

Much more is known of the trends in Irish population after 1660. The hearth-money tax returns examined by DICKSON, O GRADA & DAULTREY for the years 1676 to 1685 show that the tax yield during that time increased by 1.1 per cent per annum in Munster and by as much as 2.3 per cent per annum in Ulster. This reversal of the early seventeenth century experience can be explained by the changing patterns of immigration. The initial English enthusiasm for overseas migration was waning by the 1630s; indeed the perception that England was overpopulated was fading and emigration was being discouraged. Thus the rate of immigration to Ireland was slowing down before 1641. While there were a few bursts of English migration to Ireland in the late seventeenth century, they were minor by earlier standards. Munster in the late seventeenth century, for instance, experienced little new settlement from south-west England, which had been its main source of supply of settlers in the earlier part of the century. Instead, to achieve population growth the province had to rely principally on the natural increase of its population.

Few seventeenth-century parish records survive, so it is difficult to estimate trends in birth or death rates or the incidence of marriage in Munster or elsewhere. One group, the Quakers, did register births, marriages and burials and their Irish records have been analysed and compared with those of Quakers in England by D.E.C. EVERSLEY. Between 1650 and 1699 the marriage age among Irish Quakers was certainly lower than among their English counterparts. This gave Irish Quaker women a longer child-bearing period. Thus fertility rates were higher among Irish Quakers than English Quakers. Irish fertility rates were further enhanced by the shorter interval between recorded births. The result was a larger completed family size among Irish Quakers—a completed family size of 5.4 compared with 4.0 in England. On the mortality side of the equation Irish Quaker infant mortality seems to have been lower than in England at this period and Irish Quakers generally could expect to live up to two years longer than their English counterparts.

How typical of Irish society as a whole these findings are remains unclear. Valerie MORGAN'S analysis of the Church of Ireland parish register of Blaris in south Antrim has shown that between 1661 and 1700 baptisms were running at 150.2 per annum and burials at 55.2. The population of this prosperous parish was increasing naturally at a rapid rate. The number of marriages in the parish also rose from an average of 25.7 per annum in 1661-7 to 34.3 per annum in 1681-9. Such rapid household formation, with a low age of first marriage, might be expected in a society characterised by high immigration (mainly of young unmarried people) and by relatively easy access to land for the support of new families. Thus the age profile of the community would be skewed towards youth, and births for a period would far outnumber deaths.

CULLEN (1981) has suggested that dietary changes in Ireland during the seventeenth century may have led to a fall in the death rate. Other general health factors may also have played a part. Most visitors to Ireland commented on how free of disease it was and plague was a rare visitor. There was only one major outbreak of plague in the sixteenth century, in 1574-7, and two in the seventeenth, 1604-6 and 1649-53.

Natural increase, brought about by a high birth rate and possibly, though more uncertainly, by a falling death rate, combined with limited net immigration, were the key factors in the growth of population in late seventeenth-century Munster. We know less about the situation at that stage in Leinster and Connacht but the trend of faster population growth in the eastern part of Ireland than in the west, already evident by the 1660s, was reinforced in the later seventeenth century. As J.H. ANDREWS has demonstrated for the 1690s, the bulk of the population lay southeast of a line extending from Belfast to Limerick. In Restoration Ulster, all the Munster growth factors were in evidence, the major difference being that immigration in the north continued to be the dominant engine of population growth. The later 1650s had seen a dramatic influx of settlers, mainly into east Ulster. This migration slowed down in the early 1660s, but in the later part of the decade and in the 1670s it speeded up again. Religious difficulties in Scotland, notably Covenanter disturbances, ensured continued migration to Ireland. Some of this settlement was undone by migration back to Scotland and England, with the economic depression from 1685 and the political problems of 1689-91. The 1690s, however, saw a final great surge of Scottish movement into Ulster; a result of very severe harvest failure in Scotland which had little effect in Ireland. One contemporary estimated that between 1690 and 1696 some 30,000 Scots had come to Ulster and that following the harvest failure of 1696 another 20,000 came in that year alone. Disastrous harvests in 1698 and 1699 encouraged further migration on a lesser scale from Scotland.

As Philip ROBINSON has pointed out this immigration was different from that which had occurred earlier in the century.

Much of the earlier migration was landlord-sponsored: landlords had tried to attract suitable tenants to settle their newly acquired estates. From the 1660s the pattern of settlement was more that of a colonial spread. Thus it was the areas in the immediate hinterlands of the main ports of entry into Ulster that were most heavily settled.

As in Munster at an earlier stage, rising population reduced settler opportunity in Ulster and emigration, undetectable earlier, was occurring by the 1680s. Ulster-based Presbyterians, for instance, began to show an interest in the New World. The scale of this emigration is difficult to determine but the evidence of the Quaker records, though a very small sample, is suggestive. These show 39 people leaving Ireland for Pennsylvania in the 1680s of which 16 were from Ulster and only 5 from Munster. In the 1690s only 3 Quakers left Ireland for Pennsylvania but this rose to 26 in the first decade of the eighteenth century.

II

Within the context of rising population occurred the second significant dynamic of change: the redistribution of landed resources and property rights between natives and newcomers. In 1550 most of the land of Ireland was held by Catholic lords of either native Irish or Anglo-Irish origin. By 1600 there had already been significant transfers of land to mainly Protestant New English settlers even in areas outside formal plantation schemes such as Connacht. J.G. SIMMS has estimated that by 1641 the Catholic landowners' share stood at about 61 per cent of Irish profitable land. By 1688 this had fallen to 27 per cent and by 1703 it reached 15 per cent. This eclipse of the Catholic landlords is usually ascribed to the plantations of the sixteenth and early seventeenth centuries and to the Cromwellian and Williamite confiscations. Undoubtedly these had an immediate impact but their significance should not be overestimated. The sixteenth-century settlements of Laois-Offaly in the midlands and Newry in south Ulster were not intended as exercises in land transfer. They were political expedients, mainly military settlements to defend the pale, and their effect was localised. The plantations of Munster in the 1580s and of Ulster in the early seventeenth century were more thorough but they were also reactions to political events—the execution of the earl of Desmond and the flight of the earls respectively. While these schemes were carefully planned, the limited resources of government proved unable to enforce them fully or to police the activities of those granted forfeit land. Many who received land were more concerned to establish themselves as local magnates than to promote the political aims of the plantation schemes.

Plantation projects proved to be an ineffective method for transforming the landowning elite. Only in Ulster, the most rigorously managed of all the colonial settlements, did the percentage of land owned by Catholics fall below 50 per cent by 1641. After a series of failures during the 1620s in the Irish midlands and Wentworth's disastrous attempt to plant Connacht in the 1630s, the policy of full-scale plantation was abandoned. The settlements of the mid- and later seventeenth century differed from the earlier schemes in that they did not require the new grantees to introduce settler tenants or to create a veneer of English 'civility' by building towns or enclosing land. These later settlements were straightforward confiscations of land from those on the losing side following war or rebellion. They had a profound effect on the pattern of landholding since they speeded up a trend towards the creation of larger estates already evident earlier in the century. GILLESPIE (1987b) has shown that the Cromwellian settlement in Mayo, for example, eliminated many of the smaller freeholders and created more manageable estates which were to form the basis for future economic development.

Even more important than changing the identity of the landowners was the way in which the various settlements of the sixteenth and seventeenth centuries changed the nature of property rights in Ireland. Both NICHOLLS and O'DOWD (1986, 1988) have pointed out the variety of methods of landholding in Gaelic Ireland during the sixteenth century. Broadly speaking, land was not held in great estates by lords but was held individually by large numbers of freeholders, the lord holding only his mensal land. This freehold land was subject to partible inheritance and ownership often became fragmented. In some circumstances the expansion of dominant lineages at the expense of declining groups helped to bond divided parcels of land together.

The link between a Gaelic lord and his followers did not take the form of leases or land grants. The links were bonds of service and loyalty, freeholders paying a tribute to the overlord in return for protection and the services of the lordship, such as arbitration. As CANNY (1971) has shown, this relationship was changing by the end of the sixteenth century as the warlords began to transform themselves into *de facto* landlords, levying rents on their followers. Plantations and informal settlements accelerated this trend, though as late as the 1640s some parts of the country, such as Tipperary, had a bewildering complexity of different types of tenures operating side by side.

The spread of a common-law system of property rights, based on grants from the king and leases to tenants rather than on Gaelic social coventions had three major economic effects. First, it opened the possibility of a market in land with property changing hands for money with relatively few obstacles. This had been the case in the late sixteenth century near the major port towns, such as Galway, Waterford and Dublin, where merchants had sought to become landowners as part of their ascent on the social scale. In 1586, for example, it was complained that in Galway 'many merchants...have relinquished their mansions in towns and keep themselves in the country'. This process accelerated in the seventeenth century. The 1622 commissioners complained that 'the merchants here in all the cities of the kingdom do as they grow unto wealth withdraw themselves into the country and there settle upon farms and neglect their trade of merchandise in which they were bred.'[7]

The merchants were not the only group to benefit economically from the extension of royal authority and new tenures. The Old English gentry also began to purchase large quantities of land outside the pale both for themselves and their younger sons. By 1641, for example, Old English interests in the counties of Sligo and Roscommon, where they had possessed little land in 1600, accounted for 21 and 20 per cent of profitable land respectively. New English settlers were also building up large estates by purchase and mortgage from the native Irish. In Munster the most spectacularly successful cases were Richard Boyle, first earl of Cork, whose methods have been illuminated by Terence RANGER, and Sir Philip Perceval who used his income as a royal official to finance his acquisitions. Indeed the most successful colonisation scheme of the early seventeenth century, the settlement of Antrim and Down, was managed entirely through purchases of land by private individuals of recent English and Scottish origin from native Irish lords.

This opportunity to buy land from the native Irish began in the late sixteenth century because of the Irish lords growing indebtedness. The Nine Years War had placed a considerable strain on the resources of Irish lords who had hired large numbers of expensive Scottish mercenaries. By 1603, for example, O'Donnell had mortgaged a considerable amount of his land to a group of Dublin merchants and O'Neill had also mortgaged lands to Dublin men. Many natives became further indebted during the early seventeenth century and mortgaged yet more land to newcomers. In County Cavan, for example, the amount of land owned by native Irish fell from 22 per cent to 16 per cent between 1609 and 1641, and in Armagh over the same period it fell from 25 per cent to 19 per cent. In the non-planted county of Monaghan the trend was similar with native-Irish owned land falling from 60 per cent to 40 per cent at the same time. This increasing indebtedness was an important element in the growing frustrations among the Ulster Irish leaders, described by GILLESPIE (1986a), which fuelled rebellion in 1641. The ten years of war which followed the rebellion made it impossible for mortgagors to redeem the earlier mortgages. Much land therefore passed irrevocably into the hands of newcomers and of Old English, although the position of the latter was considerably undermined subsequently in the Cromwellian and later land settlements.

The second economic consequence of the spread of English style property arrangements was the creation of a standard system of landholding throughout the whole island. Land, held by the landlord under a grant from the king, was now set to tenants by lease or other agreement made between landlord and tenant. This delimited the role and property rights of the landlord and of the central government. Under the native Irish system the local lord was sovereign in his own country. Merchants could trade in areas under a Gaelic lord's jurisdiction only if they made their own arrangements with individual lords. Customs duties were levied by individual lords on goods or fishing rights as they saw fit. Economic activity involving more than one lordship thus involved negotiation and organisation at considerable cost, and few merchants had been willing to undertake such a task. These local property rights in customs and taxation were not the sole preserve of the native magnates since the main port towns claimed similar trading rights. The resumption of these rights by the crown as part of the general farm of the Irish customs in 1613, described by Victor TREADWELL (1978), and the limiting of landlords' property rights, played a vitally important part in opening Ireland up to greater trading activity in the seventeenth century insofar as the transaction costs of wholesale trade were substantially reduced for merchants.

The third economic consequence of the new system of property rights was a more careful definition of private property. Land now commanded a price and hence the rights associated with it had to be more carefully delimited. The second session of Charles I's 1635 parliament enacted a comprehensive body of land law to safeguard those rights. This was supplemented in the course of the century culminating in the statute of frauds of 1695 which laid the basis of modern Irish conveyancing law. The two commissions of defective titles in the early part of the century were as much about defining and safeguarding title for landowners as about raising revenue for the crown. There was also much discussion about setting up a central registry of title to land which would make conveyancing easier. Lord Deputy Wentworth proposed such a move in the 1630s and in the 1680s William Petty drew up a detailed plan for the establishment of such a registry. This more precise attitude to land title may also have played some part in the gradual abandonment by the native Irish of the practice of gavelkind, a system which had given rise to considerable fragmentation of landownership with unending disputes over property rights and boundaries.

At the local level, delineation of boundaries became more important than before. As ROBINSON has shown, most of the property units of the seventeenth century, such as the townland and barony, were taken over intact from the native Irish system, the townland becoming the basic unit for leasing. Only the county unit was an innovation in most of the country, introduced mainly for the purposes of local government. Boundaries, hitherto fluid, became fixed and more clearly defined when they were document-ed in leases and in official records such as the Civil and Down surveys. The need for clearer definition prompted the rise of a new profession: the estate surveyor. Estate maps such as those made in 1625 by Thomas Raven for the Clandeboy estate in county Down and in 1634 for the Essex estate in Monaghan were an integral part of the exploitation of newly defined property rights.

Thus the transfer of control over resources from natives to newcomers and the reorganisation of property rights in matters such as taxation and trade changed the economic face of Ireland. New-found property rights were safeguarded through statute law and through more precise definition, thereby opening the way to their exploitation in new ways. Such a change was of central importance in the successful attraction of settlers to Ireland.

III

Another fundamental and interlocking dynamic of change was an alteration in the way economic life was organised. In the early sixteenth century the economy of Ireland, outside the pale and east Munster, and the social arrangements on which it rested, was essentially redistributive in character. The surpluses generated by the economy were, in the main, disposed of not through markets or as rent payments but through food 'renders' and tributes paid by freeholders and lesser lords to greater lords. In return, the tribute-receiving lords provided services such as military protec-tion and the administration of justice, and redistributed the food collected through guesting and feasting as described by Katharine SIMMS (1978). Society was held together by ties of obligation and had few formal market structures or towns. Of course this system did not operate in a pure form. Gaelic Irish lords did trade with other areas, and some of the surplus food collected by them was sold to the 'grey merchants' from the pale towns. However such trade was localised, and the vast bulk of Irish overseas trade in the sixteenth century was probably not conducted through the large towns but through 'havens', of which contemporaries noted many. Here foreign merchants who had agreements with individual lords could exchange wine, salt and iron for some of the lordship's surplus. Native lords were not unfamiliar with coin or monetary values as frequent references to different coin types appear in Gaelic documents recording obligations of lesser lords to greater, such as the Ceart Ui Neill, demonstrate. The use of money was most prevalent in areas which had frequent contact with the pale, and by the end of the fifteenth century some market towns in areas such as Longford and Cavan had begun to flourish, and O'Reilly had gone as far as to strike his own coinage.

By contrast the economic system understood by the settlers used markets to a much greater extent. Land was not vested in the freeholders but in landlords and the use of that land was determined by a price—the rent. The surplus produce of this economic system was redistributed through the market at a price governed by the laws of supply and demand. The cohesive force in this society was wholesale trade mediated through a series of local markets and possibly extending through a hierarchy of towns into the world of international commerce. The expansion of this system into native Irish areas during the late sixteenth and early seventeenth centuries meant that the economy became increasingly commercialised. 'Markets increase commerce' wrote one contemporary, 'and procures one produce to be brought to sale for the buying of another, which tends that [he] that hath access to the market shall be more readily furnished with commodities wherein to employ his money and so the seller is furnished with money to buy.'[8] Trade was, of course, regulated by law, whether grants of market rights, control of customs or regulation of property rights. Sale through legally recognised markets also protected property rights since it made stolen goods more difficult to trade.

Just as the native redistributive system did not exist in its pure form in the mid-sixteenth century, the market or commercial system into which Ireland was drawn during the seventeenth century was still underdeveloped by 1700. Economic factors, such as a shortage of suitable tenants, acted as a constraint on landlords from charging the full economic rent for holdings during the seventeenth century. As GILLESPIE (1988a) has shown, landlord-tenant relations were governed by factors other than economic ones. There were institutional controls on economic agents. The idea of creating a new 'commonwealth' was strong among early seventeenth-century landlords and their tenants. It would be easy to write off as propaganda the earl of Cork's description of his clearance of woodland in early seventeenth century Munster as 'commonwealth work', yet that was one element underlying his motivation. Woodland clearance deprived potential rebels of a haven. In building up the iron works, which used the timber for fuel, Boyle was creating employment and wealth which prevented settlers from falling into poverty at a time when an increasing agricultural population was beginning to press on resources. Many other seventeenth-century landlords embarked on similar projects for the same reasons. Most settlers believed in the idea articulated by one of them that 'as idleness procureth poverty so poverty breedeth discontent'.[9] To provide labour was not only to create wealth but to contribute to public order and the good of the commonwealth. The church also encouraged this, and good-neighbourliness was enjoined on members of the Church of Ireland by the 1615 Articles of Religion. More practical action was taken by the church in limiting the rates of interest to be charged on money, usurers being threatened with prosecution in the ecclesiastical courts. In the towns, guilds also promoted a sense of community which served to reduce the impulse to maximise profit and some urban corporations tried to regulate prices. The government also approved of this action and attempted to control interest rates in an act of 1635. In times of shortage the government tried to control supplies and prices.

The ideas of 'redistributive' and 'market' economies are best regarded as poles on a spectrum along which Ireland moved some way during the seventeenth century. The pace of change differed from region to region and some areas lagged far behind, as GILLESPIE (1987b) has argued, but by the end of the century all areas of the country had been affected. By the 1660s rents were almost universally paid in cash, indicating that tenants had access to markets or fairs in order to sell their produce. Indeed as early as the 1630s cash was the normal way of paying rent and it was only in some marginal areas, such as Fermanagh and Mayo, that rent in kind was still being collected. The late seventeenth century saw an even greater need for cash as regular taxation, such as the hearth money, was normally rendered in coin. During the seventeenth century the idea of a commonwealth was gradually replaced among the landowning class by a more market-orienated view of the economy. Symptomatic of this were the economic prescriptions for Ireland put forward by William Petty in his *Political Anatomy of Ireland* written about 1672. Even the Baptist Richard Lawrence could not rely solely on a moral case to denounce the practice of swearing. Instead he used an economic argument, estimating that it cost the Irish economy £20,000 a year. He made similar estimates of the cost of other vices such as gambling and drunkenness. Many native Irish had difficulty in adjusting to the new market-driven system. By the 1660s, 90 per cent of all British settlers in Ulster lived no more than five miles from a market centre. The native Irish tended to live further away. Some native Irish moved into marginal areas which market forces had hardly penetrated, giving rise to distinctive regional societies such as that along the Ulster-Leinster border described by GILLESPIE (1989b).

IV

The shift in the relative importance of the two economic systems had profound implications for the Irish economy. Produce, previously consumed by lords and their households, was brought into the network of markets and much of it re-sold into a wider world through the multiple transactions of merchants. It was this development which lay behind the trade boom which characterised early seventeenth-century Ireland in particular. Donald WOODWARD (1989) has attempted to measure the extent of this commercialisation by using trade data. In 1640-1, for example, at least 1.5 million and possibly over 2 million sheep were being exported from Ireland in various forms. One of the most important elements in this trade was wool, especially from the commercialised areas of Munster. Again the strong growth in the cattle trade, with 45,000 live cattle being exported in the year before the 1641 rebellion, points to a high level of commercialisation. This trade boom was achieved through the foundation of new market towns and the re-birth of old ones. Between 1600 and 1649 over 500 grants were made specifically authorising the holding of new markets. Another 130 were added between 1660 and 1690. In addition to these regular markets there were seasonal fairs for trade, especially for the sale of cattle. By 1684, according to Bourke's *Almanac*, there were 503 fairs operating in the country. Many of these early grants were speculative ventures and there were complaints in the 1635 parliament of excessive tolls being charged by patent holders in a hurry to recoup their investment in market grants and the infrastructure of the marketplace. GILLESPIE (1990) has shown that many early establishments failed and that others changed the authorised dates of the market or fair to suit local conditions.

Along with the growth of markets and fairs in the seventeenth century, the port towns expanded dramatically to cope with the new volume of wholesale trade. Belfast and Derry were new seventeenth-century creations, the former being regarded as the second largest port in Ireland by the end of the century. While this was not so, the fact that contemporaries believed the claim points to the scale of its growth. R.J. HUNTER has illustrated the relatively slow growth of towns such as Derry in their early years, although Derry grew much faster in the second half of the seventeenth century. Cork grew from about 2,400 people in 1600 to almost 5,500 in 1641 and probably about 10,000 by the 1680s. Its outports of Youghal and Kinsale grew even more dramatically. Limerick and Waterford probably doubled their population over the century.

However the most dramatic growth over the century was that of Dublin, growing from about 5,000 people in 1600 to perhaps 45,000 in 1685 and to 62,000 by 1706. This growth in population was matched by an expansion in Dublin's share of the Irish trade despite the fact that the city was endowed with a dangerous harbour. In 1616-17 Dublin's share in the Irish customs was 21 per cent. By 1630 that had grown to almost 33 per cent and by 1662-3 it was nearly 47 per cent. By the beginning of the eighteenth century it stood at almost 50 per cent. Dublin pushed its influence north and west. By the 1640s Dublin was exporting a large number of Ulster cattle, and it is significant that in the late seventeenth century the Ulster linen trade was carried on not through the Ulster ports of Belfast or Derry but through Dublin. In the south, Cork managed to hold its position, its share of the customs revenue of the country growing from 9 per cent in 1616-17 to over 12 per cent by 1681-2.

This rapid growth of Dublin illustrates an important tendency in the increasingly commercialised economy of the seventeenth century. Sixteenth-century economic activity outside the pale had been organised mainly on a lordship basis, whereas by the end of the seventeenth century the beginnings of a nationally integrated economy were emerging with regions showing signs of specialisation. There are a number of indications of this, including the growth of a internal urban network in the late seventeenth century. But the most important concrete demonstration of this was the increasing standardisation of weights and measures necessitated by growing inter-regional and international trade. There had been some attempts in the sixteenth and early seventeenth centuries to have a national standard, notably the act of 1570 (12 Eliz. c. 3), but these had not been enforced and most towns set their own standards. Towards the end of the seventeenth century English measures came to be adopted by many Irish towns as England held the largest share of Irish trade. This development culminated in an act of 1697 setting standard weights and measures for the whole country, supplemented by later acts setting specialist measures, such as those for linen sizes.

Thus by the end of the seventeenth century the structures of economic life and the social foundations on which they rested had been transformed. Commercial contract rather than status, measured by the number of a lord's followers, was rapidly becoming the measure of a man's place in society. The output of the Irish economy, as measured by the volume of trade, had increased dramatically and the beginnings of regional specialisation and large-scale international trade can be identified.

TRENDS IN THE SEVENTEENTH-CENTURY ECONOMY

I

The initial impact on the economy of the Nine Years War, which broke out in 1594, was fairly limited. Gaelic Ireland was a society well used to warfare and feuding. A man's status was traditionally measured not by his landholding but rather by the number of his followers and his wealth, which in turn was determined by his holdings of cattle. Thus, as Katharine SIMMS (1975-6) has demonstrated, warfare in the sixteenth century was not concerned with the conquest of territory or the building of castles and hence not fought through set-piece battles. Warfare consisted essentially of cattle raiding and the 'persuasion' of freeholders to accept a new lord. The early part of the Nine Years War conformed, in the main, to this pattern and so cannot be seen as unduly disruptive of the norms of Irish society. Indeed the war had some beneficial effects. While the Old English towns of the pale remained loyal to the crown there were claims that some merchants profited by supplying arms to both sides in the conflict. Any monetary effects of a reduction in trade were more than offset by the large subventions paid in coin by the London government to support the army in Ireland. A.J. SHEEHAN (1990) has calculated that the subvention from the English Exchequer in the early 1590s averaged just over £17,000 sterling per annum. By 1595-6 it was £67,360, and by 1598-9 it had reached a peak of £196,001.

However, as the war progressed and Elizabeth's determination to crush the earl of Tyrone was stiffened, hostilities became more severe and the economic dislocation was correspondingly greater. It was at its worst in Ulster in the years after the battle of Kinsale when Lord Mountjoy pursued his 'scorched earth' policy resulting in the wholesale destruction of crops and livestock. The effects of this were compounded by poor harvests and plague in the later years of the war so that economic dislocation lasted until 1605 even though peace was signed in 1603. This crisis in the early years of the new century was compounded by monetary chaos. In an effort to save cash London reduced its 1600-1 subvention to

Ireland to about a third of that of the previous year and compensated by debasing the Irish currency in April 1601. The new coinage, of which £307,000 face value was issued between 1601 and 1603, contained only about a quarter silver, instead of about two-thirds as previously. This proved unacceptable to the merchant community many of whom refused to accept the new coinage. There was considerable discontent, and SHEEHAN (1983) has argued that this proved a factor in the recusancy revolt in the towns in 1603. The escalation of the war after 1600 meant that the overall effect of the Nine Years War on the Irish economy was disastrous. It is difficult to quantify this, but visitation returns for the dioceses of Ferns, Leighlin, Clonfert and Kilmacduagh all show a substantial decline in the value of church livings between the late sixteenth and early seventeenth centuries—a 75 per cent fall in the case of Clonfert and Kilmacduagh.

Despite this dislocation, the economy recovered quickly. The pattern of the early seventeenth-century economy was one of expansion. Customs yields provide one indication of this. The yields of the customs are not precisely comparable over long periods of time due to revisions of rates, notably in 1632, 1637 and the early 1660s (indicated by breaks in the Graph I on p. 62). However the yields do provide evidence of the trend over time and show near continuous growth up to the 1640s. There were some reversals, notably in 1622-4, 1628-32 and 1639-41 caused by harvest and commercial crises. The scale of the expansion is illustrated by WOODWARD's (1970a, 1970b) estimates of the Irish trade through Chester, one of the main destinations for Irish exports. In the late 1580s, for example, somewhere between 25 and 60 dickers of hides (a dicker being 10 hides) were landed at Chester each year from Ireland. By 1639 this had grown to 1,289 dickers per annum. Similarly, in the late 1580s between 11 and 70 packs of yarn were landed each year which had grown to 113 packs by 1639. Tallow exports to Chester in the late sixteenth century had peaked at 50 hundredweight in 1592/3 but 619 hundredweight were landed in 1639. More spectacular was the growth in wool exports from between 100 and 200 stone in the late 1580s to 6,666 stone in 1639. Yet all these changes were dwarfed by the great success story of the early modern economy, the growth of the cattle trade from almost no regular shipments of livestock in the sixteenth century to over 15,000 beasts a year in the late 1630s. This growth in trade was not limited to Chester and can be demonstrated for most ports trading with Ireland. In the case of London the value of Irish imports (in constant 1604-Book-of-Rates values) rose from £592 in 1587/8 and £3,317 in 1601/2 to £5,883 in 1633-4. As a result of this growth the Irish balance of trade was usually substantially in surplus before 1640.

Some of the reasons for this expansion in Irish trade during the early seventeenth century have already been examined: a population growing from a low base added to the labour supply, and output expanding more rapidly than population in the early stages of growth. A shift to a more commercial economy meant that more of the country's produce was being processed through the market system. GILLESPIE (1987a) has argued that the lack of a mint in Ireland meant that the money supply was not increasing as fast as the growth in trade and hence the economy tended to be deflationary and prices low. As in the late sixteenth century this gave Ireland a competitive advantage against its trading partners. CANNY (1985) has suggested one further reason for increased output: he has argued that the differences between early seventeenth-century Ulster and Munster are explicable in terms of differing use of agricultural and manufacturing technology, which made the Munster economy more efficient than that of Ulster. GILLESPIE (1986b) has argued for a limited role for technical change in any part of the country at that stage and has suggested that the low grain yields and low carrying capacity of pasture point to the modest impact of new technology. Even if technology had made a major impact on grain yields, a greater harvest could only be achieved with an increased labour supply, since little labour-saving technology was available for harvesting before the nineteenth century.

Despite this growth in output, the overall structure of the pre-1641 economy was very similar to that of the late sixteenth century. The settlers expanded what already existed rather than transforming it radically. The composition of recorded Irish trade in 1615-16, as measured in 1666 prices, shows that cattle and cattle products accounted for about half the total value of trade. Grain exports in the early seventeenth century, at almost 6 per cent of the total, had apparently developed from a strong late sixteenth-century base. Indeed exports of grain, mainly oats, from Ulster to Scotland had reached such a scale by 1619 that a series of Scottish 'corn laws' were imposed to restrict the trade for fear of depressing the Scottish market. Fish formed about 18 per cent of Irish trade by 1616 and sheep and wool about 11 per cent. Some new items had therefore appeared in the trade returns, particularly grain. These apparent innovations reflect changes in the scale of customs duties which now encouraged the export of goods previously heavily taxed, rather than changes in the internal structure of the Irish economy.

In the early years of the seventeenth century the main development in both agriculture and trade was a move from arable farming to pasture. Live cattle became the mainstay of the Irish export trade, being sent to English graziers for fattening before final sale. The expansion in live cattle exports was dramatic. At Chester in 1607, for example, only 16 live cattle were landed from Ireland, but by 1639 some 15,814 animals were discharged at the port. The switch from arable to pasture was of such concern to contemporaries, preoccupied with feeding a growing population, that the Irish House of Commons appointed a committee in 1634 to draw up a bill to prohibit the conversion of arable land to pasture. The late sixteenth century had seen a dramatic growth in the cattle trade over much of Europe as a result of an increasing demand for meat. In England, for example, between the 1590s and the 1630s live cattle prices rose by over 50 per cent. Over the same period grain prices rose 34 per cent and the price of animal products, such as butter or meat, rose by only 22 per cent. Thus the growth of the live cattle trade within Ireland was as much a response to an external economic stimulus as an adaptation by settlers to local conditions which were particularly favourable to cattle production.

In other respects the features of the early seventeenth century economy were those of the sixteenth century writ large. Fishing, especially pilchards, continued to be of considerable importance in the Munster economy, for example. Pilchard exports more than trebled between 1616 and 1625, although they fell off later as the pilchard shoals moved from the Munster coast. Herring exports doubled between 1616 and 1641. In one respect the early seventeenth-century trade was however different. Fishing in the sixteenth century had been carried on by foreigners but in the seventeenth century those settlers who could muster enough capital to set up commercialised fishing centres in Munster led the way.

The timber trade, expanding from the 1550s, grew particularly rapidly in the early seventeenth century but it was to be a short-lived phenomenon. By the late 1630s the best timber, that used for pipestaves, was almost exhausted. Areas such as the Bann valley in Ulster, the Slaney valley in south Leinster, the Blackwater and Bandon valleys in Munster were rapidly denuded of timber. By the 1680s the number of staves exported from Ireland was about a third of the 1641 level and by the early eighteenth century Ireland had become a net importer of timber. This dramatic change reflects the 'asset stripping' character of the new order. The management of timber resources in Ireland contrasts strongly with the case in England where conservation and replacement of what was then an almost exhausted resource took priority.

The early destruction of timber was in part the result of clearances of new areas for settlement by colonists. The mature phase was associated with specific new industrial processes, notably iron working. In the sixteenth century Ireland had been a net importer of iron but between 1600 and the 1640s Ireland exported considerable quantities of iron. In part this was the result of the abundant availability of timber for the production of charcoal and also the discovery of local deposits of iron. Eileen McCracken's study of the Irish woods has shown that iron working was concentrated in areas where woodland was most dense, such as Wicklow, south Derry and parts of Munster. Within these areas the furnaces tended to be located near rivers or on the coast as the transport of such a bulky product was only viable by water. What gave the expansion of iron working its impetus was the settlers' desire for profit. An agent on the Conway estate in county Antrim advised his master in the 1620s that although an iron works would cost £1,000 to set up it would yield as much in profit within a year. In fact such expectations were rarely justified. Richard Boyle, first earl of Cork, who became the largest iron master in early seventeenth-century Ireland ran his works at a considerable loss for many years before profit was attained. RANGER has shown that even then the profit was modest. Between 1607 and 1643 Boyle expended some £70,000 on his iron works while receiving only £95,000 in return. Boyle had an ulterior motive in maintaining his works as they provided him with goods to sell in England and elsewhere. This allowed him build up credits in England which could be drawn down on visits there. In effect he used the trade as a means of moving money in an era when no regular banking mechanism existed to perform this function.

Despite Boyle's experience in the iron trade he had no lack of imitators. Many early seventeenth-century settlers regarded Ireland as an attractive source of short-term profit and attempted to establish industrial concerns there. Sir Thomas Roper, later Lord Baltinglass, began his Irish career by setting up profitable fisheries at Schull, Crookhaven and Bantry. By the 1630s he felt further profit could be made in the cloth trade and established a centre near Dublin to produce well-dressed, coloured cloth. The enterprise failed because his product was too expensive for the domestic market and he lacked the commercial contacts to sell it abroad successfully. Similarly there were several attempts to establish woollen manufactories in early seventeenth-century Munster where a number of English clothiers had settled. Much of the wool produced there was suitable for working up into broadcloth, bays and new draperies, but in practice most of it was exported unworked or in the form of heavy cheap cloths such as frieze. The woollen trade experienced particular technical problems. It was not profitable to produce fine woollens since the export from England of fuller's earth, necessary for finishing, was prohibited and it was not available locally. Although the output of Irish wool was small by English standards it helped to guarantee that the cloth manufacture in England was kept at full stretch. Government regulations tried to ensure that raw Irish wool was sent to England rather than to Europe. A system of staple ports for wool exports was established and in the 1630s a licensing system was enforced.

These endeavours by individuals were matched by central government attempts to develop a manufacturing base in Ireland.

Schemes for the midland plantations, for instance, required the settlers to plant flax in the hope of encouraging the development of a linen industry. Monopolies were also granted, especially in the 1630s, for mineral prospecting. This not only raised money for the Exchequer but also encouraged searches for minerals such as silver and alum. The most strenuous attempts in this area were made during the lord deputyship of Thomas Wentworth and have been described by Hugh KEARNEY (1959). Wentworth attempted to develop the production of linen cloth by restricting the export of linen yarn in the hope that it would be worked up into cloth. Such faith did he show in this scheme that he personally directed the importation of flax seed from Holland and set up about seven looms manned by workmen from France and the Low Countries. At his trial in the 1640s Wentworth claimed the enterprise had personally cost him £3,000. However, as had been the case in the 1570s, these attempts had little success in promoting cloth manufacture. While exports of unworked linen yarn fell in 1636-7, by 1638 they exceeded the 1635 level.

Attempts to diversify the early seventeenth-century economy had little national impact but left their mark on some regions, most noticeably on the estates of the earl of Cork where viable manufacturing enterprises were carried on. There were at least three structural reasons for the very limited success in the diversification of the economy in the early seventeenth century: lack of skills, lack of capital, and a poor marketing structure. The sixteenth-century problem of a skill shortage continued to plague the Irish economy. The immigration which occurred in the late sixteenth and early seventeenth centuries had been selective and newcomers were mostly drawn from among those seeking land rather than people seeking employment. Land in Ireland was cheap and, at least until the early years of the seventeenth century, readily available, especially in Ulster where the sixteenth century population levels had been lowest. It was difficult to persuade settlers to live in towns and concentrate on craft occupations. Immigrant skilled artisans could expect to make a resonable living but the low cost of land meant that the rent or income which could be expected from it were vastly greater than could be earned from practising a craft. Richard Boyle made £25,000 profit on his iron works between 1607 and 1643 but this was only about two year's rental from his estate. The return on capital employed makes the contrast even clearer: £70,000 had been invested in ironworking, while his land had been acquired through crown grants at almost no direct cost. Those who took leases of land could reasonably hope to sell the lease for a considerable profit after a few years. By contrast the urban evidence examined by CULLEN, SMOUT & GIBSON suggests that real wages in Dublin before 1640 were not significantly higher than in Scotland. As a result there was little incentive for skilled craftsmen to settle in Ireland or if they did they saw greater potential in farming than in continuing to exercise their craft. It was only when land became increasingly difficult and expensive to obtain in the late seventeenth century that this pattern began to change. Some landlords, such as the earl of Thomond who settled Dutchmen on his lands in the 1620s, tried to resolve this difficulty by attracting men with special skills to their estates through the offer of strong inducements. While such settlements had local significance they had little overall impact on the supply of skills in the economy. The training of native Irish in certain crafts also helped to ease some local shortages but this happened to such a limited degree that it had little overall impact.

In theory, a skill shortage should have resulted in a rise in real wages to attract craftsmen. But this would only hold true if there was a substantial demand for their labour. In fact, demand was limited because an individual's ability to set up new manufactories was severely constrained by other factors limiting diversification.

The second constraint on diversification lay in the fact that while many of the new developments were capital intensive there was a shortage of capital in Ireland. One estimate of the cost of setting up a cloth works in Munster in the 1610s set the figure at between £2,000 and £3,000. An attempt by Thomas Wilson failed because he was unable to raise the capital. A pilchard fishery was no less capital intensive with start-up costs of at least £1,000 (mainly for nets and boats). In Munster, Richard Boyle made interest free loans to his tenants for small projects but the ready funds available to him, as one of the richest men in the British Isles, were available to few other Irish landlords. The Irish economy was severely undercapitalised in the early seventeenth century and high interest rates made borrowing almost impossible. Only a landlord like Boyle could invest large capital sums in wool and iron and be prepared to wait some time for a return on his investment.

The third constraint on diversification was that of marketing. Trade in unprocessed agricultural goods was a relatively simple matter but finding a market for luxury goods such as fine linens or high quality woollen cloth was much more difficult. Thomas Roper's experience with high quality cloth manufacture points to the difficulty of vending such goods in Ireland. More sophisticated marketing techniques were needed than were available among the limited merchant community in Ireland. Richard Boyle identified this problem and attempted to solve it by making contacts in continental Europe to sell his goods. His main agent was one John Quarles who sold his Munster cloth in the Netherlands, where the finishing processes were carried out. Such activities by isolated individuals, while important in local terms, never made a significant impact on the economy as a whole. The inland marketing system, although growing rapidly, remained relatively unsophisticated and was not backed up by an adequate credit system. The economy, as might be expected in the early years of a settlement, was undercapitalised and the settlement had not attracted the sort of skills necessary for diversification or significant regional specialisation.

II

Despite these problems the general picture of the Irish economy in the early seventeenth century is of steady expansion in terms of primary exports, and probably of output, based on a few main staples: live cattle, timber and grain. However, the late 1630s saw a downturn in the Irish economy. A series of poor harvests made the general economic situation difficult and the mysterious movement of the pilchard shoals away from the Munster coast deprived that region of one of its staples. In Ulster the political problems of the late 1630s exacerbated the economic difficulties so that the downturn there was probably worse than in other areas as GILLESPIE (1986a) has suggested. Against this regional background the outbreak of war in 1641 compounded existing problems.

The regional impact of the war is difficult to measure but it seems to have hit Ulster harder than most other areas. It was Ulster which saw the greatest and most disruptive military activity during the early years of the war. In general, the east of the province seems to have been more seriously affected than the west. East coast trade was orientated towards England which was also at war after 1642. One port book for the early months of 1649 for Chester, a key port for Dublin trade, indicates that the import of cattle and wool had come to a halt and that the hide trade was operating at less than one-twelfth of the 1639 level. Sheepskin imports from Ireland were less than a quarter those of 1639. The trade of the ports of the south-east, south and west of Ireland was also badly hit. The import of Irish wool at the three main English ports for the Munster trade (Barnstaple, Minehead and Dartmouth) fell from 10,356 hundredweight per annum in the mid-1630s to 506 hundredweight in 1646-7. Barrelled beef imports were halved and the tallow trade had fallen to a third of its earlier level. These estimates from English port books may well overstate the fall in the trade since smuggling probably increased during the war years. Trade with continental Europe from these ports still continued and may have offset some of the fall in the English trade. It is also clear that other types of less formal trade grew. Jane OOHLMEYER, for instance, has pointed out the upsurge of privateering, particularly in the Wexford area, the profits of which clearly provided a boost to the local economy. It is not possible to measure the scale of this, admittedly erratic, activity but it was clearly significant locally. One ship, for example, brought in prizes worth £1,500 and between February 1648 and February 1649 another brought in prizes worth about £8,000. But whatever the regional pattern the general level of trade was considerably reduced in these years. Falling exports meant a reduction in the supply of coin and several attempts were made to rectify the situation by melting down local plate and issuing coin locally, but this had only a limited degree of success.

The problems of war in the 1640s were compounded by the outbreak of plague in 1649 which continued sporadically until

1653. The early 1650s were extremely difficult years in general for the Irish economy. The ratio of English subventions to Irish revenue, for instance, in the years 1649-56 almost equalled that of the years 1598-1602 when the Nine Years War was at its height. In particular livestock levels which had suffered badly throughout the war of the 1640s were greatly reduced by 1650. Prohibitions had to be placed on the export of hides, beef, pork, cattle and tallow in the early 1650s in order to conserve stocks. Specific imports were exempted from custom duties in order to help the restocking of the country.

From the middle of the 1650s there were signs of an improvement in the Irish economy. Good harvests in 1657 and 1659 resulted in a surge of exports. By 1658/9 the number of Irish ships entering the port of Bristol reached 70 per cent of the pre-war boom years of 1636/7. In the late 1650s the London government began to reduce its subvention to the Irish exchequer as revenues increased. Property prices also rose. The rents charged by the state for confiscated Catholic property in towns increased by 23 per cent between 1654 and 1656-7, and by a further 5 per cent by 1659. CULLEN (1976) has also detected evidence of improving living standards for what was a reduced population.

The depression of the 1640s had been regional in its effects and so was the recovery. The share of taxation borne by the individual provinces within Ireland provide one indication of the regional differentials. By 1659, Ulster, probably the worst affected region in the 1640s, was paying almost 25 per cent of the national taxation burden, a slightly higher proportion than in 1634. GILLESPIE (1988b) has suggested that this was a direct result of the impact of Scottish and English immigration during the 1650s. This in turn was a response to cheap land offered by Ulster landlords anxious to settle their estates after the war. Leinster and Connacht in 1659 were paying a lower share of national taxation than in 1634. This was probably due to the disruption of trade created by the expulsion of Catholic merchants from the port towns in 1655, described by T.C. BARNARD (1975). Significantly it was in the towns of Cork, Waterford, Galway and Limerick that the Commonwealth administration found most difficulty in disposing of confiscated property. In Dublin, relatively unaffected by the expulsion of

Catholic merchants, trade recovered rapidly in the later 1650s and provided a sound base for the city's dramatic growth in the late seventeenth century. In Munster, probably the least affected of the four provinces by the events of the 1640s, the share of taxation paid in 1659 was marginally greater than in 1634. This was due to the expansion of the colonial trade with the West Indies and America in the 1650s.

III

Much of the promise of economic progress of the late 1650s was not fulfilled. The early 1660s saw a slump in trade and in 1665-7 the country experienced a financial crisis. Confidence was undermined by the uncertainty of the Restoration land settlement and the fears created by a temporary ban on cattle exports in 1663, although these fears were short-lived. However, the 1650s had provided at least one enduring legacy. The desire to engage in empirical enquiry, to experiment and to explore new practical ideas reached Ireland through Cromwellian settlers such as William Petty. This had a tangible expression in the formation of the Dublin Philosophical Society. The development was not entirely the result of the activities of Cromwellian settlers. Earlier settlers such as Miles Symner, whose career has been examined by BARNARD (1972) were its forerunners. The new spirit was well exemplified in Gerard Boate's *Ireland's natural history* published in 1652. Boate not only described the Irish landscape but made recommendations for its improvement. Indeed as BARNARD (1975) has stressed, many of the improvements in the 1650s, such as the re-establishment of ironworks, were made by Cromwellian settlers. Thus the 1650s saw a restocking of Ireland not only with people and livestock but also with new ideas about how the economy could be developed.

The timing of this development was propitious since second-generation settlers were looking for just such ideas. The war of the 1640s had forced settlers in Ireland to make irrevocable choices as to where their future lay. Many opted to remain in Ireland where the bulk of their assets were now located. As a result they became not merely settlers in Ireland but, as contemporaries called them,

Anglo-Irish or Scots-Irish. By the end of the century this trend towards integration and identification with their new country was manifested in the emergence of a form of colonial nationalism. But already from the 1660s it is detectable in a desire to improve the state of the country economically. Treatises on improved estate management were published in Dublin for the first time. In 1673 Michael Haward's essay on cattle management was published in Dublin and, at a lower social level, many late seventeenth-century Dublin almanacs contained advice on improving agricultural practices. In addition, English literature on agricultural improvement was now circulating in Ireland.

In a more tangible and practical sense the need for agricultural change also presented itself. The demands for taxation by the central government grew dramatically in the late seventeenth century. Direct taxation in the early part of the century had consisted of irregular subsidies levied in 1615, 1635 and 1640. The war of the 1640s had required more regular income by the Confederate Assembly to maintain an army in the field, and more regular county taxes were introduced which were continued under the Commonwealth in the form of the monthly assessment. In the later part of the century regular taxation, notably the hearth tax, was introduced which required regular payments to be made by Irish householders. These new demands did not come at an opportune moment in Irish economic development. Population was rising rapidly and this was placing increasing pressure on resources, as evidenced by the considerable subdivision of holdings in some parts of Ireland, with the consequent risk of impoverishment and inability to pay taxes or rents. This risk was greater given that agricultural prices were falling throughout much of the late seventeenth century. This was particularly serious since the lack of diversification in the economy meant that landlord incomes were almost wholly dependent on rent receipts and tenant welfare on farm produce sales. This situation differed from the early seventeenth century experience in that the population was rising from a higher base and the problem was therefore more acute.

Added to the demands of central government and a growing population was the destabilisation of the Irish economy caused by the passage of the English Cattle Acts of 1663 and 1667 which, by prohibiting the import of live cattle, undermined what had evolved as the mainstay of early seventeenth-century Irish trade. It soon became clear that alternatives to this trade would have to be developed in order to prevent the growth of poverty. The greater awareness of the problem of poverty in the late seventeenth century is shown by David DICKSON's description of the evolution of poor-relief legislation which became more common than it had been earlier. The solution to the threat of poverty adopted by many landlords was to encourage with renewed vigour craft industry as a means of supplementing the incomes of farms which were diminishing in size through subdivision. The encouragement of fishing on Sir William Petty's Kerry estate, for example, was done 'forasmuch it will be an employment to the people who otherwise would be troubled to pay the rent'. In Cork towards the end of the century, Sir Richard Cox offered a similar reason for encouraging economic change.[10]

The range of projects promoted by landlords was wide but was limited by available resources. Iron production, for example, which had been developed as the staple industry in the early seventeenth century, was no longer an option since much of the woodland which provided the fuel for iron works had been exhausted. Imported timber was too expensive as a raw material for a native iron trade to compete with cheap Swedish imports. Landlords had to turn to other activities. Petty, for example, pointed out the fact that dairying was more labour intensive than simply grazing cattle since, he claimed, it required hay-making to provide winter feed. The increased availablilty of labour may have been a factor in the promotion of dairying in the late seventeenth century.

The encouragement of new forms of economic activity was dependent on the development of the internal marketing system so that new specialised local products could reach a wider world. Hence Sir John Perceval, commenting on Kanturk in 1681, noted 'the place is capable of a woollen manufacture. But be pleased to mind the fairs first'.[11] Such development was to be a cooperative venture between landlords and merchants, and local merchants had to be wooed. The agent on the Herbert estate in Kerry expressed an interest in encouraging merchants in 1683 when he noted of a Cork merchant, Thomas Wills, that he was 'a good tenant and a protestant, who, by having that concern in Lord Herbert's manor lays out considerable sums at their fairs. Such a tenant must not be slighted.'[12] In this partnership it was the role of the landlord to provide the infrastructure to attract merchants. GILLESPIE (1988a) has described this process in the Lagan valley area of Ulster where one landlord, Arthur Brownlow, estabished the manufacture of fine linens on his estate by guaranteeing to purchase all that his tenants brought to market. Later in the century the earl of Abercorn promoted the linen trade at Strabane through spinning and weaving competitions. Liam IRWIN has illustrated the activities of Roger Boyle, first earl of Orrery, in using the Munster presidency to promote economic change. Boyle developed Charleville in the 1660s as a model which he hoped others would follow, encouraging French and Dutch settlers onto his lands and providing capital to begin a linen trade. He also formed an association with a Dublin merchant, Thomas Parsons, in an attempt to form a joint stock company, the Merchant Adventurers of Munster, in 1670. Other progressive landlords attempted similar schemes, most noteably the earl of Ormond's woollen and linen manufactories at Callan, Clonmel, Carrick-on-Suir and Chapelizod, where experienced textile workers from Brabant were settled.

The degree of success of these ventures varied considerably. The picture painted of Sir William Petty's Irish estates by BARNARD (1981) is of an ambitious projector who failed. One reason for this failure seems to have been that his estates were relatively remote and hence did not attract either the number of settlers required or the necessary marketing structures to sell the fish or iron which the estates produced. Moreover Petty's chief concern was speculative and as a result the schemes were invariably undercapitalised. Similar failures, mainly due to the lack of cooperation between merchants and landowners, were it seems common.

IV

It would be wrong to ascribe all the changes in the late seventeenth-century economy to the activities of landlords and merchants. Increasingly in the late seventeenth century more general economic factors came to determine the produce of individual regions. It was when general trends coincided with landlord activity that the result was most successful. Late seventeenth-century price movements described by CULLEN (1968) favoured butter and wool over cattle and beef so it is hardly surprising that Irish exports moved away from live cattle to processed goods, especially butter, barrel beef and wool. The Cattle Acts of 1663 and 1667 certainly speeded up this transition but they did not initiate it. Barrel beef exports in 1665, for example, were almost twice what they had been in 1641 while live cattle exports had only increased by about 26 per cent. Similarly, pork and bacon exports became prominent for the first time in 1665. The beef and butter trade continued to expand during the late seventeenth century. The demand for the former came from the colonies while the latter was shipped mainly to northern France and Flanders. Such diversification was broadening the base of the Irish economy but it was not without its difficulties. The butter trade in particular was notoriously unstable. War with France in 1677, for example, resulted in a near collapse of the butter market since merchants were not prepared to buy butter that they could not quickly export.

It would be wrong to dismiss entirely the potential of a live cattle trade had it been permitted. During a temporary lapse in the Cattle Acts in 1679 and 1680, 8,000 and 24,000 live cattle were landed in England during the two years. However, this 1680 return was less than half the 1665 total which suggests that the switch to new forms of exports was already well established.

This trend had considerable influence on the internal organisation of the Irish economy. As long as the live cattle trade was dominant there had been little need for specialisation within the livestock trade but with the rise of the butter and provisions exports, increased regional specialisation was required. Geographical factors dictated a division between breeding and fattening areas for cattle, the latter requiring better land while breeding could be done on poorer land. East Connacht and the midlands soon became established as fattening country. Commercial dairying to produce butter and cheese developed in the hinterlands of the major ports in Ulster and south-east Ireland along with Kerry, Cork and Limerick. Lands of more marginal quality in

Roscommon, Limerick, Clare and Westmeath together with parts of Tipperary became the centres for sheep raising for the woollen trade. The beginnings of such regional specialisation was promoted not only by the trend in the economy but also the emergence of a stable marketing network which was encouraged by both landlords and merchants. As a result inland market towns began to grow, directing their trade towards Dublin, Cork or Belfast. This was paralleled by a corresponding decline in the regional port towns which had benefited from the early seventeenth-century boom.

The other main export of the late seventeenth century was wool in its various forms. However the amount of raw wool being exported in 1687 was only marginally greater than in 1665. The slow growth in this trade may reflect the high level of duties on imports to England and takes no account of the considerable smuggling to Holland, France and Spain which developed in the late seventeenth century. The dramatic expansion was in woollen cloth exports. Cloth manufacture had the distinct advantage over commercial dairying in that it needed relatively little capital to set up, an important consideration in a still under-capitalised economy. Ireland had other advantages in the cloth and wool trades. Imports of foreign cloth to England carried high duties and imports of Scottish cloth were banned in 1667. As a result the woollen industry of areas such as Chester, Lancashire and especially the Exeter region came to rely on Irish wool for their cloth and Irish wool was used as far afield as Norfolk. Ireland also filled a gap in the English market since its main product was frieze, a cheap coarse cloth intended for the lower end of the market not catered for by domestic English production. By 1695 it was estimated, with perhaps some exaggeration, that some 12,000 English settlers were employed in woollen manufacture in Dublin and 50,000 in the country as a whole. Indeed economic conditions in Ireland following the Williamite wars were so favourable that the serge makers in the English West Country were beginning to move to Ireland before the trade was interrupted by the Woollen Act of 1699.

Price movements and landlord encouragement were crucial in these developments but the opening up of new markets for Irish trade, especially after 1650, was also crucial. In 1665 about 74 per cent of all Irish exports were destined for England. By 1683 this had fallen to 30 per cent; by 1700 the English share of Irish trade had risen moderately to 42 per cent. One market which was exploited more intensively than before was continental Europe. In 1683, for example, France took over 20 per cent of Irish butter exports, mainly from Ulster and Munster. Belfast and Youghal between them accounted for 47 per cent of the Irish butter trade by 1683. It was through this European trade that Ireland was able to run a balance of payments deficit with England. D.W. JONES has estimated that the Irish balance of payments deficit with England in 1685-6 was about £260,000 which was funded by a £214,000 balance of payments surplus with continental Europe. As the continental trade declined in the 1690s this balance almost totally dissappeared.

Another market which absorbed an increasing proportion of Irish trade was the trans-Atlantic trade to the West Indies and the American colonies. Between 1683 and 1685 almost 61 per cent of Irish barrel beef and pork exports went to America as did more than a quarter of cheese exports. The West Indian sugar islands, for example, had their main source of beef and butter in Ireland. From the 1650s Galway was exporting significant quantities of provisions to the West Indies and prominent Galway merchant families, such as the Blakes, Lynches, Kirwans, Frenchs and Skerrets, became important figures in the Carribbean economy. From the 1660s the centre of the trans-Atlantic trade moved from Galway to Cork which exported about half the Irish total of beef sold to the colonies. The 1680s saw further expansion in the trade as labour shortages in the American colonies drove prices of colonially produced goods upwards making Irish imports more competitive. Thus trade expanded rapidly in the late seventeenth century and was interrupted only by the Williamite wars.

Despite this growth Thomas TRUXES has estimated that the balance of trade between Ireland and America in the late seventeenth century favoured the American colonies. This resulted from rising living standards in Ireland and the increased demand for luxury items supplied by the colonies, especially tobacco. Irish imports of tobacco, for example, rose from 1,817,775 pounds in 1665 to an average of 2,850,193 pounds a year between 1683 and

1686. CULLEN (1976) has estimated that by the 1680s Irish tobacco consumption per capita was at a level not exceeded until the second half of the nineteenth century. By 1700 tobacco imports stood at 3,281,645 pounds. These are, of course, the official figures; the real imports when smuggling is allowed for were considerably higher. The growth in wine imports was also significant, rising from 1,500 tuns in 1614-5 to an average of 2,200 tuns a year between 1683 and 1686. The distribution of this growing prosperity among the population is still a matter for speculation. The fall in prices of food items, such as grain and meat, gave wage earners greater discretionary expenditure as a smaller proportion of their incomes was spent on food. Thus, real wages among Dublin labourers rose dramatically in the latter part of the century. The position of primary producers is less clear but price falls were probably offset for many tenants by the growing volume of output which maintained incomes.

This was a potentially perilous situation: prosperity dependent on continued expansion of output as prices drifted downwards. However, two exceptionally good harvests in 1686 and 1687, while increasing exports, drove prices down to unrealistic levels. In 1688 disease hit cattle. The 1688 customs yield fell dramatically. This economic difficulty was exacerbated by the worsening political crisis. Protestant landlords and merchants fearful of James II's intentions in Ireland, began to leave the country taking with them their goods, and, more especially, their cash. Set against this political and economic crisis, the effects of the 'war of the two kings' in 1689-91 was greater than a simple analysis of the war might suggest. As in the 1640s, the effects were regional with Ulster bearing the brunt both of the fighting and the economic dislocation. A comparison of the hearth tax yields before and after the war shows that the areas most affected were western Ulster and the north midlands whereas the south-eastern counties were relatively little affected. However the effects of the war on Ulster were over by late 1690 whereas in Munster the war lasted well into 1691, and the army were still quartered there in 1692 thus creating further dislocation. A comparison of the Perceval estates in Cork and Kildare shows that in Cork by 1693 the rental had not recovered to the 1688 level whereas in Kildare it was 20 per cent above that of four years previously.

What is remarkable about the 1690s is the speed of recovery from the war. One factor which may account for this was the absence of plague, in contrast to the 1650s. Another factor was the rapid resettlement of most of the country after the war. The capital inflow which accompanied this funded a high level of imports in the first half of the 1690s which were required to rebuild the economy. For instance livestock had again been seriously depleted; in 1691 exports of beef and pork were prohibited for six months but the trade was resumed in 1692, although it was 1697 before the trade attained its pre-war level. However it was not cattle which were central to the recovery but cereals: there was a dramatic growth in grain exports at a time of European harvest crises. Grain production had been a prominent feature of the domestic economy of late seventeenth-century Ireland. Limerick, Kildare, Meath, Waterford and the counties on the east coast were noted as important grain growing areas before the war and Ulster produced considerable quantities of oats and barley. However this production had not been reflected in the export figures because grain exports were retarded by low international prices due to good European harvests before the 1690s. Increased grain output had also been used to feed the growing urban population, although production may have run ahead of domestic needs. According to one contemporary calculation Dublin accounted by 1680 for about 9 per cent of the Irish population whereas, around 1600 it had represented less than 1 per cent of the population. It is hardly surprising that the areas closest to it should be among the most important grain-producing areas. By 1700, however, grain formed a greater proportion of Irish exports than it had in the 1660s. In part this switch from cattle to grain was the response to price movements abroad. A comparison of the 1680s with the 1690s in England, for example, shows that livestock prices increased by 11 per cent and livestock products by 13 per cent, but grain rose by 20 per cent. This abundance of grain in Ireland, together with cheap land, available as a result of emigration from Ireland during the crisis of the late 1680s, served to attract a new influx of settlers in the 1690s. The harvest crises of the mid-1690s in Scotland prompted a considerable movement of Scots into Ulster. Certainly by 1700 rent levels in both Ulster and Munster were up to or beyond those of the boom years of the 1680s.

V

The experience of the seventeenth-century economy was one of significant change conditioned by a number of autonomous factors. The arrival of English and Scottish settlers and new marketing practices early in the century prompted a dramatic expansion from the low base of the underdeveloped sixteenth-century economy but there was relatively little change in the composition of its output. Increased labour inputs expanded the output of a traditional economy. As the settlements developed, and landlords began to realise new opportunities for profit and the need to diversify the economic structure to cope with the demands of central government and an expanding population, so they began to change the structure of the economy. They utilised the newly emerging market system to their own advantage and in doing so they encouraged its growth. New industries, such as the weaving of fine linens and the processing of agricultural produce, became a more important part of that economy. These changes were not solely engineered by landlords since increasingly in the second half of the century the signals provided through the market, in the form of price movements, came to dictate what would be produced. In this way the economy became more specialised and regional markets developed. Dublin gradually emerged as the centre for these markets. Other external factors, such as government legislation, were also at work in promoting change but their role, as we shall see, was limited. The seventeenth-century Irish economy underwent a process of maturation which went hand in hand with the social maturation of the various settlements.

THE LIMITS TO CHANGE

Impressive though the speed and scale of change in the seventeenth-century Irish economy may have been, it is important to remember that such changes took place within a framework which imposed limits on that change. Some of these limits arose from the nature of the economy itself, such as the financial system that evolved to service the economy, and others from outside the economy, such as governmental legislation shaped by the economic ideas of the day. Of these ideas the most important and pervasive were those which have been christened by later historians as mercantilist. The term is not easily defined; it was first used to describe a set of ideas and policy prescriptions relating to the capacity of the state to manipulate international trade and the balance of payments as a way of protecting and enhancing national prosperity. Thus the response to commercial or industrial difficulty in any branch of the seventeenth-century English economy was couched in mercantilist terms: sectoral depression led directly to the demand for protection or other trade restrictions in the form of legislation or order in council. These ideas had their effect on Ireland, as KEARNEY (1958) has shown, and resulted in enactments discriminating against some Irish products, such as cattle and wool, and in restrictions on the use of Irish shipping in certain colonial trades.

Historians imbued with nationalist sentiments writing at the beginning of the twentieth century, such as George O'BRIEN, have seen such policies as part of an integrated campaign to destroy Irish trade and any signs of Irish commercial rivalry. Set in a seventeenth-century context such legislation turns out to have been inspired by the panic fears of pressure groups and lobbies in England who blamed Irish trade and competition during the times of English trade depression, the causes of which were often far more complex. Patrick KELLY has shown that the Woollen Act of 1699, which prohibited Irish exports of wool, was not the result of English government policy and that its passage was, in fact,

51

contrary to the wishes of the then administration. The political history of the Cattle Acts of 1663 and 1667 have been described by WOODWARD (1973) and C.A. EDIE. They have shown that the English parliament was exclusively concerned with circumstances in the English regions. The impact on Ireland was, in a political sense, quite incidental. From 1660 falling cattle and cereal prices in England had caused uproar among cattle producers there and they had begun to agitate for restriction of cattle shipments from Ireland and Scotland. The result was a victory for the English breeders over the English graziers who bought in mature stock and who had opposed the cattle bill. The act of 1663 took effect in 1664. Far from improving the situation in England conditions for cattle farmers became worse in the next four years, the main reason being the outbreak of the Anglo-Dutch war in 1665. As a desperate move, the English market for Irish sheep, cattle and pork was completely closed by the Westminister parliament in February 1667, against the wishes of the English administration. This was not the first attempt to restrict imports of Irish cattle into England. During the trade depression of 1621 there had been moves in the English parliament by West Country cattle graziers to have Irish cattle imports banned. These had come to nothing and evaporated with the recovery of English trade.

Not all legislation affecting Ireland was the product of panic. In the early seventeenth century there had been a deliberate attempt to limit the Irish export trade in wool through the creation of a system of staple ports, described by George O'BRIEN (1926). This policy was really a continuation of the legislation of 1522 and 1537 which had sought to prohibit unregulated Irish wool exports, replacing it by a licensing system in the 1570s. More comprehensive were the attempts by Lord Deputy Wentworth in the 1630s, detailed by KEARNEY(1959), to reduce wool exports and to encourage a linen industry in Ireland but these had little effect. More serious for Irish trade were the restrictions on imports contained in the Navigation Acts of 1660 and 1671 and the Staple Act of 1663, codified in the Navigation Act of 1696 and examined by Thomas TRUXES. These acts required that certain items from the colonies could not be landed directly in Ireland but had to be shipped to England for re-export to Ireland. Thus one of the staples of the trade of Whitehaven and Liverpool became the re-export of tobacco to Ireland. The main effect of this was to increase prices of imports from the colonies. One estimate of 1686 suggested that the restrictive terms of the acts added half a penny to the price of every pound of tobacco sold in Ireland (about 8 per cent of its cost). The result was apparently a considerable rise in smuggling, although this is impossible to quantify. Certainly by the 1680s Irish ships were using the Isle of Man as a base for smuggling operations involving tobacco. The London government was sufficiently worried about the scale of smuggling operations to investigate. They bought out the customs rights of the island from their owner. London control however did not come about until 1765.

More serious than legislation in limiting economic change was the structure of the economy itself and its social base, in particular the shortage of capital and of an adequate credit system to compensate for this shortage. From the earliest stages of British settlement in Ireland the London government had been aware of the need to attract 'men of substance' as settlers, men who would have the resources to develop their newly acquired estates. Unfortunately the great magnates of Tudor and Stuart England and Scotland had not, in the main, shown great interest in acquiring Irish land. Those who were attracted by the prospect of cheap land and quick profit were men with few assets to support them. They were usually younger sons, those rising on the social scale or those descending in status who saw in Ireland a chance to retrieve their fortunes. As Sir Arthur Chichester said of the Ulster planters in 1610, 'those from England are, for the most part, plain country gentlemen... If they have any money they keep it close for hitherto they have disbursed little... The Scottish come with greater part and better accompanied, but it may be with less money in their purses.'[13]

Those from within Ireland who got land in the various plantation schemes usually had only the limited profits of royal office to disburse on their estates. Thus many had to set land on long leases with high entry fines (initial payments by tenants which were discounted against future rent payments) in order to raise immediate cash to begin developing the infrastructure of their estates. As a result they put themselves into the perilous financial situation which Peter ROEBUCK has described. Even for those who did not resort to these techniques, rents were difficult to increase in the short term since the low population levels of the early seventeenth century meant that competition between landlords was for tenants rather than among tenants for land. The result was a system of landlord-tenant relations, described by GILLESPIE (1988a), which were conditioned by non-economic considerations. Landlord finances throughout the seventeenth century were dependent on regular rent payments. When these stopped, as they did during the 1640s, many found themselves in an impossible position and had to resort to the sale of their estates. Only landlords with a very large rental income, such as the first earl of Cork (£12,000 a year in the 1630s), had the capital reserves to withstand such a prolonged crisis. This situation was not confined to landlords. Many of their potential tenants who came to Ireland had little cash to develop their holdings, and for landlords there was a continual problem of finding good quality tenants.

This situation could have been overcome had there been a well-developed credit system which would allow landlords to borrow in order to finance estate improvements with such borrowings being serviced by rising rental incomes. No such credit system existed, and Michael MACCARTHY MORROGH (1987) has demonstrated the difficulties of borrowing. The groups in the early modern world who usually had cash in hand to lend, clergy, merchants and lawyers, were of little help to landlords in Ireland since these groups also were deploying their surplus in the land market. Moreover their surplus was usually small. Ireland's trade was, in the main, carried in the hands of foreign merchants and on foreign ships. A late sixteenth-century commentator noted that 'there be many merchants of the staple in the country, whereof the most are buyers and the smallest number shippers'.[14] By 1698 two-thirds of the tonnage of ships engaged in Irish trade with England were English. Outside the main towns of the pale an indigenous merchant community was almost non-existent. Where local merchants did emerge they were generally small scale operators. Lewis Roberts, in the 1630s, noted the scarcity of Irish merchants and another commentator observed in 1683 that 'the merchants generally throughout the kingdom drive a peddling trade upon credit, having not stock of their own'.[15] Richard Lawrence in the same decade echoed these disparaging comments. Studies of the cattle trade lend some credence to these comments showing that individual cargoes tended to be small and many so-called merchants shipped only one cargo a year.

This reality is also indicated by the relatively small proportion of national wealth concentrated in the towns. Dublin, for example, carrying on over 30 per cent of trade was only assessed for 2.4 per cent of the 1634 subsidy and 4.4 per cent of the 1662 subsidy. Cork was the next wealthiest town in 1634 with 1.8 per cent of the subsidy and Waterford paid 1.5 per cent, falling to 0.7 per cent by 1662. By the end of the seventeenth century the situation had begun to change. Land which had been readily available early in the century at low rates was becoming more expensive and difficult to obtain. The land market began to stabilise and fewer non-landowners had the possibility of purchasing estates and, as a result, resident merchant communities began to develop in many of the rapidly growing towns.

These problems of a shortage of lenders were compounded by difficulties inherent in the Irish monetary system. The rapid expansion of the seventeenth-century economy gave rise to an increasing number of transactions involving, for example, traders and rent payments. If there was to be no change in the price level or the velocity of circulation of money, then the supply of money had to be increased in line with the growth in the number of transactions. However, since seventeenth-century Ireland had no mint it was dependent on imported metal coin as the main means of exchange, and this was only assured if there was a favourable balance of trade. Consequently the money supply was very unstable. Coin was sometimes abundant but more often was in short supply, as the early seventeenth-century English merchant Christopher Lowther (whose experience has been described by D.R. HAINSWORTH) found when visiting Dublin. As a result barter was often resorted to. Sir Henry Sidney, for example, described how Gascony wine was being sold in Carrickfergus during the 1570s for nineteen cow skins a hogshead. Likewise, the inhabitants of Wicklow in the late sixteenth century bartered firewood for bread in Dublin. As late as the 1660s there were allegations that

Irish merchants shipping wool to England were accepting goods rather than money in return for the wool.

There were various attempts to ease this situation. From the mid-1640s local traders struck their own tokens in an effort to rectify the scarce supply of small change but with only a limited degree of success. Far more disastrous was the attempt by James II to rectify the situation by establishing a mint in Dublin in 1689 which produced brass and bronze money to replace the silver, copper and gold coin taken out of the country by refugees. Coin with the designated value of over £1 million was minted, far more than the economy in its depressed state actually required; the result was that monetary inflation became a feature of the late 1680s. This was followed by a severe deflation in the 1690s as the coinage adjusted to normal requirements.

Some of the consequences of this perilous monetary situation have been described by GILLESPIE (1989a). An adequate supply of coin being directly tied to the performance of Irish exports meant that a harvest crisis or an outbreak of cattle disease would have severe knock-on effects. Exports would fall and the balance of trade move into deficit. The external supply of coin would diminish and a commercial crisis would quickly follow a natural one. Such events were not uncommon in the seventeenth century. There were at least four major harvest crises in the early seventeenth century each of which caused considerable dislocation in the economy. In the later part of the century there were fewer major crises. Apart from that of the early 1650s, the years 1660, 1665, 1671-4 and the late 1680s stand out as periods of economic distress in Ireland.

A second consequence of the shortage of cash and credit was abnormally high interest rates. Rates of between 30 per cent and 40 per cent per annum were not unusual in the early part of the seventeenth century. Thus a shortage of working capital drove up interest rates and reduced yet further the scope for borrowing. One alternative was to borrow on foreign markets, such as London where rates were relatively low. Irish land did not prove an acceptable security in these markets because of what was perceived to be its low and unstable value. This situation was eased in the later part of the century when the expansion and diversification of trade put more cash in the hands of Irish merchants. The merchants were less willing to invest in land at high prices and turned instead to money lending. This improvement in the availability of loans pushed down the interest rate so that Sir Robert Southwell could comment in 1684 that 'money is grown so plentiful and land so scarce that although the legal interest rate there be ten per cent yet everybody upon reasonable security is content with eight'.[16]

If the financial economy was finely balanced, so too was the real economy. While the population, and hence the labour supply, had increased dramatically in the seventeenth century it was still low in relation to available resources. William Petty estimated in the 1670s that Ireland could carry five million people. He reckoned that the actual population was about two million. Labour was therefore always a scarce commodity. Skill shortages, as we have already seen, were one of the main constraining factors in the development of Irish industry in the seventeenth century. The supply of all categories of labour was problematic and could be subject to severe disruption. The political difficulties of both the late 1630s and late 1680s were compounded by economic crises which were undoubtedly exacerbated by emigration on such a scale that crops could not be harvested.

The seventeenth-century economy displayed not only a strong propensity for expansion but also had inherent limits to that change. Labour and capital were both in short supply in relation to the resources available for exploitation. A fluid land market prompted those who had capital to invest to buy land, often speculatively, at low rates rather than to lend to newly established settlers. The problem of credit was further complicated by the monetary problems. In comparison with these fundamental difficulties the restrictions imposed on economic change by legislation were of less importance.

CONCLUSION

If viewed from a standpoint at the end of the eighteenth century, the economy of Ireland in 1700 would have appeared crude and undeveloped in many respects. The countryside was by later standards sparsely populated and to the eyes of most vistors to the country it exhibited many signs of poverty. This was despite the fact that in the course of the seventeenth century Ireland's economy had grown faster than that of Scotland or France. Irish output still comprised mainly unprocessed agricultural goods, and the volume of trade was less than a fifth of the 1800 level. Services such as banking and insurance were almost non-existent. But all of this should not detract from the very significant advances which had been made during the seventeenth century. Population in 1700 was still low in relation to available resources. However the Irish population had probably grown by about one per cent per annum during the seventeenth century despite the setbacks of the crisis of the 1640s and 1650s. Much of this had been achieved through immigration, a movement which ceased at the end of the seventeenth century, leaving the Irish economy to make structural changes early in the next century to accommodate itself to a different population dynamic.

Perhaps more significantly, the seventeenth century had seen a fundamental change in the allocation of property rights. Ireland in the sixteenth century had comprised a series of largely autonomous lordships, each with its own arrangements for trade and taxation. As English royal authority expanded, these rights had been re-arranged with one authority, the crown, taking responsibility for trading arrangements and land allocation. In this way the structures necessary for a market economy were created. Indeed there are many signs that Ireland was moving in this direction even before the arrival of large numbers of settlers in the seventeenth century. Native Irish lords were making use of opportunities in the sixteenth century to extinguish the rights of freeholders and to make themselves landlords rather than warlords. The willingness with which many Gaelic lords had

entered surrender and regrant arrangements with the crown in
the sixteenth century is but one indication of this. Rather than
fundamentally changing the direction in which Irish society was
moving the events of the seventeenth century only speeded up a
process already under way. That process made possible the
integration of the national economy, the beginnings of which are
detectable by the end of the seventeenth century with the increasing domination by Dublin.

All of these changes manifested themselves in a variety of ways.
The increase in the volume of trade over the century by over 200
per cent is one measure. Another indication is the rise in land
values. In the 1620s land was changing hands at eight or nine
years' purchase (a capital value nine times the rental income). By
the early 1630s it had risen to ten years purchase and at its peak in
the mid-1630s twenty years purchase was being demanded. The
crisis of the 1640s and 1650s had pushed land prices down, in
some cases to only three years purchase, but by 1661 it had risen
again to seven years and by 1685 fifteen years purchase was asked
for. Underlying this rise in land values was a rise in rental income
for landlords. Sir William Petty confidently estimated that the total
rental of the country rose from £900,000 in 1672 to £1,200,000 in
1687.

In this assessment of growth and change it is important to bear
in mind that there were limits to the possibilities of change: a
shortage of capital, a shortage of people, a shortage of credit and
often a dire shortage of coin. Limits were also imposed from
outside, in the form of English government legislation. However
within these limits the performance of the Irish economy in the
seventeenth-century was remarkable.

The role of colonisation in this pattern of economic change
raises the question of the significance of the wider context for
interpreting Irish economic change in the seventeenth century.
Should the pattern of development be seen in the context of
changes in the European economies or as part of an Atlantic
colonial world as CANNY (1988) has outlined. Many of the
problems experienced in the various regions of colonial America
were similar to those in Ireland. Labour shortages and credit
problems were common to both regions and legislative restrictions

were also applied to both. However, the solutions adopted to these problems were often radically different. Ireland, for example, never had recourse to indentured labour or slavery to solve its labour problem. One reason for the adoption of different solutions to similar problems lies in the fact that sixteenth-century Ireland was not the virtual *tabula rasa* which the early explorers discovered in America. An economic structure based on trade with continental Europe and with England existed in sixteenth-century Ireland, and was extended in the seventeenth century. The historic pattern of Irish trade shaped its later development, whereas American-centred trade, partly because of the distances involved, evolved differently. For example, the lack of native shipping in Ireland could be compensated for by the proximity of English or European shipping whereas this was totally impractical in America and a substantial merchant marine and ship-owning community developed there. Again in urban life profound differences between the two regions emerged which have been described by GILLESPIE (1984).

If Ireland does not fit into a New World pattern, neither does it entirely suit the Old World one. Ireland did not experience the dramatic inflation of early modern Europe which resulted in at least some redistribution of wealth and may have contributed to phenomena as diverse as the witch craze and the English civil war. In contrast, Europe did not experience the social revolution which occurred in Ireland as a consequence of the redistribution of property rights and property ownership in the sixteenth and seventeenth centuries. In economic terms the expansion of trade as a result of new settlement meant that Ireland grew more dramatically than, for instance, Scotland in the seventeenth century. The Irish experience does not fit into neat models. Rather it illustrates the ways in which a variety of social groups, each with diverse religious, cultural and political backgrounds, sought their economic salvation under differing geographical and demographic conditions. To interpret the long-term evolution of the Irish economy requires an understanding of how those groups achieved economic salvation in the years before 1700.

NOTES

[1] F.J. Fisher, 'The Sixteenth and Seventeenth Centuries: The Dark Ages in English Economic History ?', *Economica*, n.s., XXIV (1951), p.18.

[2] Coggan's account is *in Calendar of Carew Mss, 1603-24*, pp.174-6.

[3] British Library, Harley Ms 3292, f.30.

[4] Marquess of Lansdowne, *Petty-Southwell Correspondence, 1676-87* (London, 1928), p.163.

[5] B.E. Howells (ed), *Elizabethan Pembrokeshire: The Evidence of George Owen* (Haverfordwest, 1973), p.3.

[6] Public Record Office, London, SP63/32/61.

[7] Brendan O Bric, 'Galway Townsmen as the Owners of Land in Connacht, 1585-1641' M.A. thesis, University College, Galway, 1974, p.708; British Library, Additional Ms 4756, f.31^v.

[8] *Calendar of Carew Mss, 1603-24*, p.205.

[9] British Library, Royal Ms 18 A LXV, f.1.

[10] T.C. Barnard, 'Fishing in Seventeenth-Century Kerry: The Experience of Sir William Petty', *Journal of the Kerry Archaeological and Historical Society*, XIV (1981), p.24.

[11] Historical Manuscripts Commission, *Report on the Manuscripts of the Earl of Egmont* (London, 1909), II, p.85.

[12] W.J. Smith (ed.), *Herbert Correspondence* (Cardiff, 1968), p.283.

[13] *Calendar of State Papers, Ireland, 1608-10*, pp.525-6.

[14] A.F.O'D. Alexander (ed.), 'The O'Kane Papers', *Analecta Hibernica* no.12 (1943), p.76.

[15] Historical Manuscripts Commission, *Calendar of the Manuscripts of the Marquess of Ormonde* (11 vols, London, 1895-1920), n.s., VII, p.136.

[16] British Library, Egerton Ms 917, f.89^v.

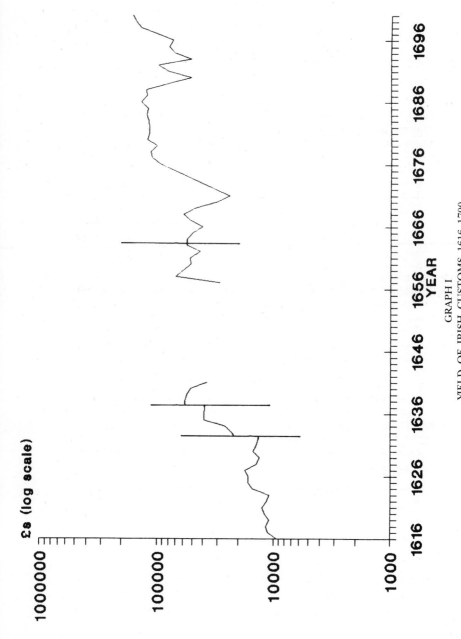

GRAPH I

YIELD OF IRISH CUSTOMS 1616–1700

SELECT BIBLIOGRAPHY

ANDREWS, J. H. 'Notes on the Historical Geography of the Irish Iron Industry', *Irish Geography*, III no. 3 (1956), pp. 139-49. Still valuable with a long-term perspective.

— — — —, 'Geography and Government in Elizabethan Ireland' in Nicholas Stephens and R. E. Glasscock (eds.), *Irish Geographical Studies in Honour of E.E. Evans* (Belfast, 1970), pp. 178-91.

— — — —, 'Land and People c. 1685' in MOODY, MARTIN, BYRNE (eds.) (1976), pp. 454-508.

— — — —, *Plantation Acres* (Belfast,1985). A history of land surveyors and mapping of which chapters 1 to 5 have some important insights for the changing perceptions of land in Ireland.

BARNARD, T. C. 'Myles Symner and the New Learning in Seventeenth-Century Ireland', *Journal of Royal Society of Antiquaries of Ireland*, CII (1972), pp. 129-42.

— — — —, *Cromwellian Ireland* (Oxford, 1975). A useful analysis of government, trade and finance for a confused period.

— — — —, 'Sir William Petty, Irish Landowner' in H. Lloyd Jones *et. al* (eds.), *History and Imagination* (London, 1981), pp. 201-17.

— — — —. 'Fishing in Seventeenth-century Kerry: The Experience of Sir William Petty', *Journal of the Kerry Archaeological and Historical Society*, XIV (1981), pp. 14-25.

— — — —, 'An Anglo-Irish Industrial Enterprise: Iron Making at Enniscorthy, Co. Wexford, 1657-92', *Proceedings of the Royal Irish Academy*, LXXXV (1985), pp. 101-44.

BUTLIN, R. A. 'The Population of Dublin in the Late Seventeenth Century', *Irish Geography* V no. 2 (1965), pp. 51-66.

CANNY, N. P. 'Hugh O'Neill and the Changing Face of Gaelic Ulster', *Studia Hibernica*, X (1971), pp. 7-35. A valuable case study of the dynamic of change in a Gaelic lordship.

CANNY, N. P. *The Elizabethan Conquest of Ireland: A Pattern Established* (Hassocks, 1976). Chapter 1 provides a general overview of Irish society in the sixteenth century.

— — — —, 'Migration and Opportunity', *Irish Economic and Social History*, XII (1985), pp. 7-32. See reply in GILLESPIE (1986b).

— — — —, *Kingdom and Colony: Ireland in the Atlantic World, 1560-1800* (Baltimore, 1988).

CLARKE, AIDAN. 'The Irish Economy. 1600-60', in MOODY, MARTIN, BYRNE, (eds.), (1976), pp. 168-86.

CULLEN, L. M. *Anglo-Irish Trade, 1660-1800* (Manchester, 1968). A pioneering work. Late seventeenth-century trade is dealt with in chapter 2.

— — — —, 'Population Trends in Seventeenth Century Ireland', *Economic and Social Review*, VI (1974-5), pp. 149-65. The best set of population estimates available with a discussion of their economic implications.

— — — —, 'Economic Trends 1660-1690', in MOODY, MARTIN, BYRNE (eds.) (1976), pp. 387-407.

— — — —, 'Population Growth and Diet, 1600-1800' in J. M. Goldstrom & L. A. Clarkson (eds.), *Irish Population, Economy and Society. . .* (Oxford, 1981), pp. 89-112.

CULLEN, L. M., SMOUT, T. C. & GIBSON, A. 'Wages and Comparative Development in Ireland and Scotland, 1565-1780', in R. Mitchison & P. Roebuck (eds.), *Economy and Society in Scotland and Ireland, 1500-1939* (Edinburgh, 1988), pp. 105-116.

DICKSON, David. 'In Search of the Old Irish Poor Law' in R. Mitchison, P. Roebuck (eds.), *Economy and Society in Scotland and Ireland, 1500-1939* (Edinburgh, 1988), pp. 149-59.

DICKSON, D., Ó GRÁDA, C., & DAULTREY, S. 'Hearth Tax, Household Size and Irish Population Change, 1672-1821', *Proceedings of the Royal Irish Academy*, LXXXII, sect. C (1982), pp. 125-81.

DUFFY, P. J. 'Patterns of Landownership in Gaelic Monaghan in the Late Sixteenth Century', *Clogher Record* X (1979-81), pp. 304-22.

— — — —, 'The Territorial Organisation of Gaelic Landownership and its Transformation in County Monaghan, 1591-1640', *Irish Geography*, XIV (1981), pp. 1-26. Two studies of the breakup of 'native' patterns of landownership in an unplanted county.

EDIE, C. A. 'The Irish Cattle Bills: a Study in Restoration Politics', *Transactions of the American Philosophical Society*, n.s. LX (1970), pp. 5-66.

ELLIS, S. G. 'Economic Problems of the Church: Why the Reformation Failed in Ireland', *Journal of Ecclesiastical History*, XLI (1990), pp. 239-65.

EVERSLEY, D. E. C. 'The Demography of the Irish Quakers, 1650-1850' in J. M. Goldstrom & L. A. Clarkson (eds.), *Irish Population, Economy and Society*. . . (Oxford, 1981), pp. 57-88.

GILLESPIE, Raymond. 'The Origins and Development of an Ulster Urban Network', *Irish Historical Studies*, XXIV, 93 (1984), pp. 15-29.

— — — —, (1985), *Colonial Ulster* (Cork, 1985). A detailed study of the settlement of Antrim and Down in the early seventeenth century.

— — — —, (1986a), 'The End of an Era: Ulster and the Outbreak of the 1641 Rising' in C. Brady & R. Gillespie (eds.), *Natives and Newcomers: Essays on the Making of Irish Colonial Society* (Dublin, 1986), pp. 191-241.

— — — —, (1986b), 'Migration and Opportunity: a Comment', *Irish Economic and Social History*, XIII (1986), pp. 90-5.

— — — —, (1987a), 'Peter French's Petition for an Irish Mint, 1619', *Irish Historical Studies*, XXV, 100, (1987), pp. 413-20.

— — — —, (1987b), 'Lords and Commons in Seventeenth-Century Mayo' in R. Gillespie & G. Moran (eds.), *'A Various Country': Essays in Mayo History 1500-1900* (Westport, 1987), pp.44-66.

GILLESPIE, Raymond. (1988a) *Settlement and Survival on an Ulster Estate: The Brownlow Leasebook, 1667-1711* (Belfast, 1988). Text and analysis of an important estate document.

— — — —, (1988b), 'Landed Society and the Interegnum in Scotland and Ireland' in R. Mitchison & P. Roebuck (eds.), *Economy and Society in Scotland and Ireland, 1500-1939* (Edinburgh, 1988), pp. 38-47.

— — — —, (1989a), 'Meal and Money: The Harvest Crisis of 1621-4 and the Irish Economy' in E. M. Crawford (ed.), *Famine: The Irish Experience, 900-1900* (Edinburgh, 1989), pp. 75-95. Deals with the commercial and monetary implications of a harvest crisis.

— — — —, (1989b), 'The Transformation of the Borderlands, 1600-1700' in R. Gillespie & H. O'Sullivan (eds), *The Borderlands: Essays on the History of the Ulster-Leinster Border* (Belfast, 1989), pp. 75-92.

— — — —, 'The Small Towns of Ulster, 1600-1700', *Ulster Folklife*, XXXVI (1990), pp. 32-42.

GRAHAM, Jean M. 'Rural Society in Connacht, 1600-1640' in Nicholas Stephens & R. E. Glasscock (eds.), *Irish Geographical Studies in Honour of E. E. Evans* (Belfast, 1970), pp. 192-208. A detailed examination of Irish landholding and agricultural practices in transition.

HAINSWORTH, D. R. 'Christopher Lowther's Canary Adventure: A Merchant Venturer in Dublin, 1632-3', *Irish Economic and Social History*, II (1975), pp. 22-34.

HUNTER, R. J. 'Ulster Plantation Towns, 1609-41', in D. W. Harkness & Mary O'Dowd (eds.), *The Town in Ireland: Historical Studies XIII* (Belfast, 1981), pp. 55-80.

IRWIN, Liam. 'The Role of the Presidency in the Economic Development of Munster, 1660-72', *Journal of the Cork Historical and Archaeological Society*, LXXXII (1977), pp. 102-114.

JONES, D.W. *War and Economy in the Age of William III and Marlborough* (Oxford, 1988). Especially useful on the 'Irish balance' of the 1680s.

KEARNEY, H. F. *Strafford in Ireland, 1633-41* (Manchester, 1959). Still the standard work. Chapters 4 and 11 deal with royal finance and Wentworth's economic policies respectively.

— — — —, 'Mercantilism in Ireland', *Historical Studies I* (1958), pp. 59-68.

KELLY, Patrick. 'The Irish Woollen Export Prohibition Act of 1699: Kearney Revisited', *Irish Economic and Social History*, VII (1980), pp. 22-44.

LENNON, Colm. *The Lords of Dublin in the Age of the Reformation* (Dublin, 1989). Chapters 2 and 3 are a good description of the social and economic structure of sixteenth-century Dublin.

LONGFIELD, A. K. *Anglo-Irish Trade in the Sixteenth Century* (London, 1929).

MACCARTHY MORROGH, Michael. *The Munster Plantation* (Oxford, 1986). The definitive account of the Munster plantation.

— — — —, 'Credit and Remittance: Monetary Problems in Early Seventeenth-Century Munster', *Irish Economic and Social History*, XIV (1987), pp. 5-19.

MC CRACKEN, Eileen. *The Irish Woods Since Tudor Times* (Newtown Abbot, 1971).

MOODY, T. W., MARTIN, F. X. & BYRNE, F. J. (eds). *A New History of Ireland*, III: *Early Modern Ireland* (Oxford, 1976).

MORGAN, V. 'A Case Study of Population Change Over Two Centuries: Blaris, Lisburn, 1661-1848', *Irish Economic and Social History*, III (1976), pp. 5-16. The only study of seventeenth-century population change from parish-register data.

NICHOLLS, K. W. *Land, Law and Society in Sixteenth-Century Ireland* (Dublin, 1976). A short pamphlet central to the understanding of sixteenth-century Ireland.

O'BRIEN, G. *The Economic History of Ireland in the Seventeenth Century* (Dublin, 1919). Still the only comprehensive book of the subject but the analysis is dated.

O'BRIEN, G. 'The Irish Staple Organisation in the Reign of James I', *Economic History*, no. 1 (1926), pp. 42-56.

O'DOWD, Mary. 'Gaelic Economy and Society' in C. Brady & R. Gillespie (eds), *Natives and Newcomers: Essays on the Making of Irish Colonial Society* (Dublin, 1986), pp. 120-47. A good introduction to the Gaelic economy.

— — — —, 'Land and Lordship in Sixteenth- and Early Seventeenth-Century Ireland' in R. Mitchison & P. Roebuck (eds.), *Economy and Society in Scotland and Ireland, 1500-1939* (Edinburgh, 1988), pp. 17-26.

O'FLANAGAN, Patrick. 'Markets and Fairs in Ireland, 1600-1800: Index of Economic Development and Regional Growth', *Journal of Historical Geography*, XI (1985), pp. 364-78.

OHLMEYER, J. H. 'Irish Privateers during the Civil War', *The Mariner's Mirror*, LXXVI (1990), pp. 119-33.

O'SULLIVAN, D. 'The Exploitation of the Mines of Ireland in the Sixteenth Century', *Studies*, XXIV (1935), pp. 442-52.

QUINN, D. B. & NICHOLLS, K. W. 'Ireland in 1534', in MOODY, MARTIN, BYRNE, (eds.), (1976), pp. 1-38. A general overview of early sixteenth-century Ireland.

RANGER, Terence. 'The Career of Richard Boyle, First Earl of Cork, in Ireland, 1588-1643', (D. Phil. thesis, Oxford, 1959).

ROBINSON, Philip. *The Plantation of Ulster* (Dublin, 1984). A geographer's perspective with valuable maps.

ROEBUCK, Peter. 'The Making of an Ulster Great Estate: The Chichesters, Barons of Belfast and Viscounts of Carrickfergus, 1599-1648', *Proceedings of the Royal Irish Academy*, LXXIX, sect. C (1979), pp. 1-25.

SHEEHAN, A. J. 'The Recusancy Revolt of 1603: A Reinterpretation', *Archivium Hibernicum*, XXXVIII (1983), pp. 3-13.

— — — —, 'Irish Revenues and English Subventions', *Proceedings of the Royal Irish Academy*, XC, sect. C (1990), pp. 35-65. Provides the raw data for a study of royal finance in the reigns of Elizabeth and James I.

SIMMS, J. G. 'Land Owned by Catholics in Ireland in 1688', *Irish Historical Studies*, VII, 27 (1951), pp. 180-90.

SIMMS, Katharine. 'Warfare in the Medieval Gaelic Lordships', *Irish Sword*, XII (1975-6), pp. 98-108.

— — — —, 'Guesting and Feasting in Gaelic Ireland', *Journal of the Royal Society of Antiquaries of Ireland*, CVIII (1978), pp. 67-100.

SMYTH, W. J. 'Society and Settlement in Seventeenth-Century Ireland: The Evidence of the 1659 Census', in W. J. Smyth & Kevin Whelan (eds.), *Common Ground: Essays on the Historical Geography of Ireland* (Cork, 1988), pp. 55-83.

TREADWELL, Victor. 'The Irish Parliament of 1569-71', *Proceedings of the Royal Irish Academy*, LXV, sect. C (1966-7), pp. 55-89.

— — — —, 'The Irish Customs Administration in the Sixteenth Century', *Irish Historical Studies*, XX, 80 (1977) pp. 348-417.

— — — —, 'The Establishment of the Farm of the Irish Customs, 1603-13' *English Historical Review*, XCIII (1978), pp. 508-602.

TRUXES, T. M. *Irish American Trade, 1660-1783* (Cambridge, 1988). Chapter 1 and appendices 1 and 2 are particularly relevant.

WOODWARD, Donald, (1970a). *The Trade of Elizabethan Chester* (Hull, 1970).

— — — —, (1970b), 'The Overseas Trade of Chester, 1600-1650', *Transactions of the Historic Society of Lancashire and Cheshire*, CXXII, (1970), pp. 25-42.

— — — —, 'The Anglo-Irish Livestock Trade in the Seventeenth Century', *Irish Historical Studies*, XVIII, 72 (1973), pp. 489-523.

— — — —, 'Irish Sea Trade and Shipping From the Later Middle ages to c. 1660', in M. McCaughan & J. Appleby (eds.), *The Irish Sea: Aspects of Maritime History* (Belfast, 1989), pp. 35-44.